The Fact of a Doorframe

Poems Selected and New
1950–1984

By Adrienne Rich

THE FACT OF A DOORFRAME:
POEMS SELECTED AND NEW 1950–1984

SOURCES

A WILD PATIENCE HAS TAKEN ME THIS FAR

ON LIES, SECRETS, AND SILENCE:
SELECTED PROSE, 1966–1978

THE DREAM OF A COMMON LANGUAGE

TWENTY-ONE LOVE POEMS

OF WOMAN BORN: MOTHERHOOD
AS EXPERIENCE AND INSTITUTION

POEMS: SELECTED AND NEW, 1950–1974

DIVING INTO THE WRECK

THE WILL TO CHANGE

LEAFLETS

NECESSITIES OF LIFE

SNAPSHOTS OF A DAUGHTER-IN-LAW

THE DIAMOND CUTTERS

A CHANGE OF WORLD

The Fact of a Doorframe

means there is something to hold
onto with both hands
while slowly thrusting my forehead against the wood
and taking it away
one of the oldest motions of suffering
as Makeba sings
a courage-song for warriors
music is suffering made powerful

I think of the story
of the goose-girl who passed through the high gate
where the head of her favorite mare
was nailed to the arch
and in a human voice
If she could see thee now, thy mother's heart would break
said the head
of Falada

Now, again, poetry,
violent, arcane, common,
hewn of the commonest living substance
into archway, portal, frame
I grasp for you, your bloodstained splinters, your
ancient and stubborn poise
—as the earth trembles—
burning out from the grain

1974

ADRIENNE RICH

The Fact of a Doorframe

Poems Selected and New
1950-1984

W. W. NORTON & COMPANY
NEW YORK   LONDON

The text of this book is composed in Times Roman, with
display type set in Bodoni.

First Edition

Library of Congress Cataloging in Publication Data
Rich, Adrienne.
  The fact of a doorframe: Poems Selected and New 1950–1984
  Includes index.
  I. Title.
PS3535.I233A6   1984   811'.54   84–6107

ISBN 0-393-01905-5

ISBN 0-393-30204-0   {PBK.}

W. W. Norton & Company, Inc., 500 Fifth Avenue, New York, N. Y. 10110
W. W. Norton & Company Ltd., 37 Great Russell Street, London WC1B 3NU

1 2 3 4 5 6 7 8 9 0

for my teachers—present and gone

Contents

Foreword

The Fact of a Doorframe is a selection from nine previous books, with an additional number of uncollected and more recent poems. In any selection from over thirty years of writing, choices are problematic and can never be final. I have left out some poems that appeared in *Poems Selected and New* (1974), largely to make room for newer work and poems that have stood a longer test of time for me.

The poems in this book were written by a woman growing up and living in the fatherland of the United States of North America. One task for the nineteen- or twenty-year-old poet who wrote the earliest poems here was to learn that she was neither unique nor universal, but a person in history, a woman and not a man, a white and also Jewish inheritor of a particular Western consciousness, from the making of which most women have been excluded. The learning of poetic craft was much easier than knowing what to do with it—with the powers, temptations, privileges, potential deceptions, and two-edged weapons of language.

I have never had much belief in the idea of the poet as someone of special sensitivity or spiritual insight, who rightfully lives above and off from the ordinary general life. In writing poetry I have known both keen happiness and the worst fear—that the walls cannot be broken down, that these words will fail to enter another soul. Over the years it has seemed to me just that—the desire to be heard, to resound in another's soul—that is the impulse behind writing poems, for me. Increasingly this has meant hearing and listening to others, taking into myself the language of experience different from my own—whether in written words, or the rush and ebb of broken but stubborn conversations. I have been changed, my poems have changed, through this process, and it continues.

Again, in this collection, I thank my editor, John Benedict, for his longtime, serious, intelligent caring for each of my books over the past sixteen years.

January 1984

Adrienne Rich

From

A Change of World

1951

Storm Warnings

The glass has been falling all the afternoon,
And knowing better than the instrument
What winds are walking overhead, what zone
Of gray unrest is moving across the land,
I leave the book upon a pillowed chair
And walk from window to closed window, watching
Boughs strain against the sky

And think again, as often when the air
Moves inward toward a silent core of waiting,
How with a single purpose time has traveled
By secret currents of the undiscerned
Into this polar realm. Weather abroad
And weather in the heart alike come on
Regardless of prediction.

Between foreseeing and averting change
Lies all the mastery of elements
Which clocks and weatherglasses cannot alter.
Time in the hand is not control of time,
Nor shattered fragments of an instrument
A proof against the wind; the wind will rise,
We can only close the shutters.

I draw the curtains as the sky goes black
And set a match to candles sheathed in glass
Against the keyhole draught, the insistent whine
Of weather through the unsealed aperture.
This is our sole defense against the season;
These are the things that we have learned to do
Who live in troubled regions.

Aunt Jennifer's Tigers

Aunt Jennifer's tigers prance across a screen,
Bright topaz denizens of a world of green.
They do not fear the men beneath the tree;
They pace in sleek chivalric certainty.

Aunt Jennifer's fingers fluttering through her wool
Find even the ivory needle hard to pull.
The massive weight of Uncle's wedding band
Sits heavily upon Aunt Jennifer's hand.

When Aunt is dead, her terrified hands will lie
Still ringed with ordeals she was mastered by.
The tigers in the panel that she made
Will go on prancing, proud and unafraid.

Afterward

Now that your hopes are shamed, you stand
At last believing and resigned,
And none of us who touch your hand
Know how to give you back in kind
The words you flung when hopes were proud:
Being born to happiness
Above the asking of the crowd,
You would not take a finger less.
We who know limits now give room
To one who grows to fit her doom.

Boundary

What has happened here will do
To bite the living world in two,
Half for me and half for you.
Here at last I fix a line
Severing the world's design
Too small to hold both yours and mine.
There's enormity in a hair
Enough to lead men not to share
Narrow confines of a sphere
But put an ocean or a fence
Between two opposite intents.
A hair would span the difference.

An Unsaid Word

She who has power to call her man
From that estranged intensity
Where his mind forages alone,
Yet keeps her peace and leaves him free,
And when his thoughts to her return
Stands where he left her, still his own,
Knows this the hardest thing to learn.

At a Bach Concert

Coming by evening through the wintry city
We said that art is out of love with life.
Here we approach a love that is not pity.

This antique discipline, tenderly severe,
Renews belief in love yet masters feeling,
Asking of us a grace in what we bear.

Form is the ultimate gift that love can offer—
The vital union of necessity
With all that we desire, all that we suffer.

A too-compassionate art is half an art.
Only such proud restraining purity
Restores the else-betrayed, too-human heart.

Stepping Backward

Good-by to you whom I shall see tomorrow,
Next year and when I'm fifty; still good-by.
This is the leave we never really take.
If you were dead or gone to live in China
The event might draw your stature in my mind.
I should be forced to look upon you whole
The way we look upon the things we lose.
We see each other daily and in segments;
Parting might make us meet anew, entire.

You asked me once, and I could give no answer,
How far dare we throw off the daily ruse,
Official treacheries of face and name,
Have out our true identity? I could hazard
An answer now, if you are asking still.
We are a small and lonely human race
Showing no sign of mastering solitude
Out on this stony planet that we farm.
The most that we can do for one another
Is let our blunders and our blind mischances
Argue a certain brusque abrupt compassion.
We might as well be truthful. I should say
They're luckiest who know they're not unique;

But only art or common interchange
Can teach that kindest truth. And even art
Can only hint at what disturbed a Melville
Or calmed a Mahler's frenzy; you and I
Still look from separate windows every morning
Upon the same white daylight in the square.

And when we come into each other's rooms
Once in awhile, encumbered and self-conscious,
We hover awkwardly about the threshold
And usually regret the visit later.
Perhaps the harshest fact is, only lovers—
And once in a while two with the grace of lovers—
Unlearn that clumsiness of rare intrusion
And let each other freely come and go.
Most of us shut too quickly into cupboards
The margin-scribbled books, the dried geranium,
The penny horoscope, letters never mailed.
The door may open, but the room is altered;
Not the same room we look from night and day.

It takes a late and slowly blooming wisdom
To learn that those we marked infallible
Are tragi-comic stumblers like ourselves.
The knowledge breeds reserve. We walk on tiptoe,
Demanding more than we know how to render.
Two-edged discovery hunts us finally down;
The human act will make us real again,
And then perhaps we come to know each other.

Let us return to imperfection's school.
No longer wandering after Plato's ghost,
Seeking the garden where all fruit is flawless,
We must at last renounce that ultimate blue
And take a walk in other kinds of weather.
The sourest apple makes its wry announcement
That imperfection has a certain tang.
Maybe we shouldn't turn our pockets out
To the last crumb or lingering bit of fluff,

But all we can confess of what we are
Has in it the defeat of isolation—
If not our own, then someone's, anyway.

So I come back to saying this good-by,
A sort of ceremony of my own,
This stepping backward for another glance.
Perhaps you'll say we need no ceremony,
Because we know each other, crack and flaw,
Like two irregular stones that fit together.
Yet still good-by, because we live by inches
And only sometimes see the full dimension.
Your stature's one I want to memorize—
Your whole level of being, to impose
On any other comers, man or woman.
I'd ask them that they carry what they are
With your particular bearing, as you wear
The flaws that make you both yourself and human.

For the Conjunction of Two Planets

We smile at astrological hopes
And leave the sky to expert men
Who do not reckon horoscopes
But painfully extend their ken
In mathematical debate
With slide and photographic plate.

And yet, protest it if we will,
Some corner of the mind retains
The medieval man, who still
Keeps watch upon those starry skeins
And drives us out of doors at night
To gaze at anagrams of light.

•

Whatever register or law
Is drawn in digits for these two,
Venus and Jupiter keep their awe,
Wardens of brilliance, as they do
Their dual circuit of the west—
The brightest planet and her guest.

Is any light so proudly thrust
From darkness on our lifted faces
A sign of something we can trust,
Or is it that in starry places
We see the things we long to see
In fiery iconography?

From

The Diamond Cutters

1955

Ideal Landscape

We had to take the world as it was given:
The nursemaid sitting passive in the park
Was rarely by a changeling prince accosted.
The mornings happened similar and stark
In rooms of selfhood where we woke and lay
Watching today unfold like yesterday.

Our friends were not unearthly beautiful,
Nor spoke with tongues of gold; our lovers blundered
Now and again when most we sought perfection,
Or hid in cupboards when the heavens thundered.
The human rose to haunt us everywhere,
Raw, flawed, and asking more than we could bear.

And always time was rushing like a tram
Through streets of a foreign city, streets we saw
Opening into great and sunny squares
We could not find again, no map could show—
Never those fountains tossed in that same light,
Those gilded trees, those statues green and white.

The Tourist and the Town

San Miniato al Monte

Those clarities detached us, gave us form,
Made us like architecture. Now no more
Bemused by local mist, our edges blurred,
We knew where we began and ended. There
We were the campanile and the dome
Alive and separate in that bell-struck air,
Climate whose light reformed our random line,
Edged our intent and sharpened our desire.

13

Could it be always sᴏ: a week of sunlight,
Walks with a guidebook picking out our way
Through verbs and ruins, yet finding after all
The promised vista, once!—The light has changed
Before we can make it ours. We have no choice:
We are only tourists under that blue sky,
Reading the posters on the station wall:
Come, take a walking-trip through happiness.

There is a mystery that floats between
The tourist and the town. Imagination
Estranges it from her. She need not suffer
Or die here. It is none of her affair,
Its calm heroic vistas make no claim.
Her bargains with disaster have been sealed
In another country. Here she goes untouched,
And this is alienation. Only sometimes,
In certain towns she opens certain letters
Forwarded on from bitter origins,
That send her walking, sick and haunted, through
Mysterious and ordinary streets
That are no more than streets to walk and walk—
And then the tourist and the town are one.

To work and suffer is to be at home.
All else is scenery: the Rathaus fountain,
The skaters in the sunset on the lake
At Salzburg, or, emerging after snow,
The singular clear stars of Castellane.
To work and suffer is to come to know
The angles of a room, light in a square,
As convalescents learn the face of one
Who has watched beside them. Yours now, every street,
The noonday swarm across the bridge, the bells
Bruising the air above the crowded roofs,
The avenue of chestnut-trees, the road
To the post-office. Once upon a time
All these for you were fiction. Now, made free
You live among them. Your breath is on this air,
And you are theirs and of their mystery.

The Middle-aged

Their faces, safe as an interior
Of Holland tiles and Oriental carpet,
Where the fruit-bowl, always filled, stood in a light
Of placid afternoon—their voices' measure,
Their figures moving in the Sunday garden
To lay the tea outdoors or trim the borders,
Afflicted, haunted us. For to be young
Was always to live in other peoples' houses
Whose peace, if we sought it, had been made by others,
Was ours at second-hand and not for long.
The custom of the house, not ours, the sun
Fading the silver-blue Fortuny curtains,
The reminiscence of a Christmas party
Of fourteen years ago—all memory,
Signs of possession and of being possessed,
We tasted, tense with envy. They were so kind,
Would have given us anything; the bowl of fruit
Was filled for us, there was a room upstairs
We must call ours: but twenty years of living
They could not give. Nor did they ever speak
Of the coarse stain on that polished balustrade,
The crack in the study window, or the letters
Locked in a drawer and the key destroyed.
All to be understood by us, returning
Late, in our own time—how that peace was made,
Upon what terms, with how much left unsaid.

Living in Sin

She had thought the studio would keep itself;
no dust upon the furniture of love.
Half heresy, to wish the taps less vocal,

the panes relieved of grime. A plate of pears,
a piano with a Persian shawl, a cat
stalking the picturesque amusing mouse
had risen at his urging.
Not that at five each separate stair would writhe
under the milkman's tramp; that morning light
so coldly would delineate the scraps
of last night's cheese and three sepulchral bottles;
that on the kitchen shelf among the saucers
a pair of beetle-eyes would fix her own—
envoy from some village in the moldings . . .
Meanwhile, he, with a yawn,
sounded a dozen notes upon the keyboard,
declared it out of tune, shrugged at the mirror,
rubbed at his beard, went out for cigarettes;
while she, jeered by the minor demons,
pulled back the sheets and made the bed and found
a towel to dust the table-top,
and let the coffee-pot boil over on the stove.
By evening she was back in love again,
though not so wholly but throughout the night
she woke sometimes to feel the daylight coming
like a relentless milkman up the stairs.

Bears

Wonderful bears that walked my room all night,
Where are you gone, your sleek and fairy fur,
Your eyes' veiled imperious light?

Brown bears as rich as mocha or as musk,
White opalescent bears whose fur stood out
Electric in the deepening dusk,

And great black bears who seemed more blue than black,
More violet than blue against the dark—
Where are you now? upon what track

Mutter your muffled paws, that used to tread
So softly, surely, up the creakless stair
While I lay listening in bed?

When did I lose you? whose have you become?
Why do I wait and wait and never hear
Your thick nocturnal pacing in my room?
My bears, who keeps you now, in pride and fear?

Villa Adriana

When the colossus of the will's dominion
Wavers and shrinks upon a dying eye,
Enormous shadows sit like birds of prey,
Waiting to fall where blistered marbles lie.

But in its open pools the place already
Lay ruined, before the old king left it free.
Shattered in waters of each marble basin
He might have seen it as today we see.

Dying in discontent, he must have known
How, once mere consciousness had turned its back,
The frescoes of his appetite would crumble,
The fountains of his longing yawn and crack.

And all his genius would become a riddle,
His perfect colonnades at last attain
The incompleteness of a natural thing;
His impulse turn to mystery again.

Who sleeps, and dreams, and wakes, and sleeps again
May dream again; so in the end we come
Back to the cherished and consuming scene
As if for once the stones will not be dumb.

•

We come like dreamers searching for an answer,
Passionately in need to reconstruct
The columned roofs under the blazing sky,
The courts so open, so forever locked.

And some of us, as dreamers, excavate
Under the blanching light of sleep's high noon,
The artifacts of thought, the site of love,
Whose Hadrian has given the slip, and gone.

A Walk by the Charles

Finality broods upon the things that pass:
Persuaded by this air, the trump of doom
Might hang unsounded while the autumn gloom
Darkens the leaf and smokes the river's glass.
For nothing so susceptible to death
But on this forenoon seems to hold its breath:
The silent single oarsmen on the stream
Are always young, are rowers in a dream.
The lovers underneath the chestnut tree,
Though love is over, stand bemused to see
The season falling where no fall could be.

You oarsmen, when you row beyond the bend,
Will see the river winding to its end.
Lovers that hold the chestnut burr in hand
Will speak at last of death, will understand,
Foot-deep amid the ruinage of the year,
What smell it is that stings the gathering air.

From our evasions we are brought at last,
From all our hopes of faithfulness, to cast
One look of recognition at the sky,
The unimportant leaves that flutter by.
Why else upon this bank are we so still?
What lends us anchor but the mutable?

•

O lovers, let the bridge of your two hands
Be broken, like the mirrored bridge that bends
And shivers on the surface of the stream.
Young oarsmen, who in timeless gesture seem
Continuous, united with the tide,
Leave off your bending to the oar, and glide
Past innocence, beyond these aging bricks
To where the Charles flows in to join the Styx.

The Snow Queen

Child with a chip of mirror in his eye
Saw the world ugly, fled to plains of ice
Where beauty was the Snow Queen's promises.
Under my lids a splinter sharp as his
Has made me wish you lying dead
Whose image digs the needle deeper still.

In the deceptive province of my birth
I had seen yes turn no, the saints descend,
Their sacred faces twisted into smiles,
The stars gone lechering, the village spring
Gush mud and toads—all miracles
Befitting an incalculable age.

To love a human face was to discover
The cracks of paint and varnish on the brow;
Soon to distrust all impulses of flesh
That strews its sawdust on the chamber floor,
While at the window peer two crones
Who once were Juliet and Jessica.

No matter, since I kept a little while
One thing intact from that perversity—
Though landscapes bloomed in monstrous cubes and coils.
In you belonged simplicities of light

To mend distraction, teach the air
To shine, the stars to find their way again.

Yet here the Snow Queen's cold prodigious will
Commands me, and your face has lost its power,
Dissolving to its opposite like the rest.
Under my ribs a diamond splinter now
Sticks, and has taken root; I know
Only this frozen spear that drives me through.

The Diamond Cutters

However legendary,
The stone is still a stone,
Though it had once resisted
The weight of Africa,
The hammer-blows of time
That wear to bits of rubble
The mountain and the pebble—
But not this coldest one.

Now, you intelligence
So late dredged up from dark
Upon whose smoky walls
Bison took fumbling form
Or flint was edged on flint—
Now, careful arriviste,
Delineate at will
Incisions in the ice.

Be serious, because
The stone may have contempt
For too-familiar hands,
And because all you do
Loses or gains by this:
Respect the adversary,
Meet it with tools refined,
And thereby set your price.

•

Be hard of heart, because
The stone must leave your hand.
Although you liberate
Pure and expensive fires
Fit to enamor Shebas,
Keep your desire apart.
Love only what you do,
And not what you have done.

Be proud, when you have set
The final spoke of flame
In that prismatic wheel,
And nothing's left this day
Except to see the sun
Shine on the false and the true,
And know that Africa
Will yield you more to do.

Letter from the Land of Sinners

I write you this out of another province
That you may never see:
Country of rivers, its topography
Mutable in detail, yet always one,
Blasted in certain places, here by glaciers,
There by the work of man.

The fishers by the water have no boast
Save of their freedom; here
A man may cast a dozen kinds of lure
And think his days rewarded if he sight
Now and again the prize, unnetted, flicking
Its prism-gleams of light.

The old lord lived secluded in his park
Until the hall was burned
Years ago, by his tenants; both have learned

Better since then, and now our children run
To greet him. Quail and hunter have forgotten
The echo of the gun.

I said there are blasted places: we have kept
Their nakedness intact—
No marble to commemorate an act
Superhuman or merely rash; we know
Why they are there and why the seed that falls there
Is certain not to grow.

We keep these places as we keep the time
Scarred on our recollection
When some we loved broke from us in defection,
Or we ourselves harried to death too soon
What we could least forgo. Our memories
Recur like the old moon.

But we have made another kind of peace,
And walk where boughs are green,
Forgiven by the selves that we have been,
And learning to forgive. Our apples taste
Sweeter this year; our gates are falling down,
And need not be replaced.

The Perennial Answer

The way the world came swinging round my ears
I knew what Doctor meant the day he said,
"Take care, unless you want to join your dead;
It's time to end this battling with your years."
He knew I'd have the blackest word told straight,
Whether it was my child that couldn't live,
Or Joel's mind, thick-riddled like a sieve
With all that loving festered into hate.
Better to know the ways you are accursed,
And stand up fierce and glad to hear the worst.
The blood is charged, the back is stiffened so.

•

Well, on that day that was a day ago,
And yet so many hours and years ago
Numbered in seizures of a darkening brain,
I started up the attic stairs again—
The fifth time in the hour—not thinking then
That it was hot, but knowing the air sat stiller
Under the eaves than when the idiot killer
Hid in the Matthews barn among the hay
And all the neighbors through one August day
Waited outside with pitchforks in the sun.
Joel waited too, and when they heard the gun
Resound so flatly in the loft above
He was the one to give the door a shove
And climb the ladder. A man not made for love,
But built for violence; he would stand
Where lightning flashed and watch with eyes so wide
You thought the prongs of fire would strike inside;
Or sit with some decaying book in hand,
Reading of spirits and the evil-eyed,
And witches' sabbaths in a poisoned land.

So it was Joel that brought the fellow out,
Tarnished with hay and blood. I still can see
The eyes that Joel turned and fixed on me
When it was done—as if by rights his wife
Should go to him for having risked his life
And say—I hardly knew what thing he wanted.
I know it was a thing I never granted,
And what his mind became, from all that woe,
Those violent concerns he lived among,
Was on my head as well. I couldn't go,
I never went to him, I never clung
One moment on his breast. But I was young.

And I was cruel, a girl-bride seeing only
Her marriage as a room so strange and lonely
She looked outside for warmth. And in what fashion
Could I be vessel for that somber passion—
For Joel, decreed till death to have me all?

The tortured grandsire hanging in the hall
Depicted by a limner's crabbed hand
Seemed more a being that I could understand.
How could I help but look beyond that wall
And probe the lawful stones that built it strong
With questions sharper than a pitchfork's prong?
If Joel knew, he kept his silence long.

But Evans and I were hopeless from the start:
He, collared early by a rigorous creed,
Not man of men but man of God indeed,
Whose eye had seen damnation, and whose heart
Thrust all it knew of passion into one
Chamber of iron inscribed *Thy will be done.*
Yet sense will have revenge on one who tries
To down his senses with the brand of lies.
The road was empty from the village home,
Empty of all but us and that dark third,
The sudden Northern spring. There must be some
For whom the thrusting blood, so long deferred
In alder-stem and elm, is not the rise
Of flood in their own veins; some who can see
That green unholy dance without surprise.
I only say it has been this for me:
The time of thinnest ice, of casualty
More swift and deadly than the skater's danger.
The end of March could make me stand a stranger
On my own doorstep, and the daily shapes
Of teapot, ladle, or the china grapes
I kept in winter on the dresser shelf
Rebuked me, made me foreign to myself.

Evans beside me on that moonless road
Walked hard as if he thought behind us strode
Pursuers he had fled through weary ways.
He only said: "Where I was born and grew,
You felt the spring come on you like a daze
Slow out of February, and you knew
The thing you were contending with. But here—"

●

"Spring is a bolt of lightning on the year,"
I said, "it strikes before you feel it near."

"The change of seasons is another thing
God put on earth to try us, I believe.
As if the breaking-out of green could bring
Escape from frozen discipline, give us leave
To taste of things by will and law forbidden."

"Maybe it was the weather lost us Eden,"
I said, but faltering, and the words went by
Like flights of moths under that star-soaked sky.
And that was all. He brought me to the door;
The house was dark, but on the upper floor
A light burned in the hallway. "Joel's asleep,"
I told him, and put out my hand. His touch
Was cold as candles kept unlit in church,
And yet I felt his seeking fingers creep
About my wrist and seize it in their grip
Until they hurt me.
                    "Neither you nor I
Have lived in Eden, but they say we die
To gain that day at last. We have to live
Believing it—what else can we believe?"

"Why not believe in life?" I said, but heard
Only the sanctioned automatic word
"Eternal life—" perennial answer given
To those who ask on earth a taste of heaven.

The penalty you pay for dying last
Is facing those transactions from the past
That would detain you when you try to go.
All night last night I lay and seemed to hear
The to-and-fro of callers down below,
Even the knocker rattling on the door.
I thought the dead had heard my time was near
To meet them, and had come to tell me so;
But not a footstep sounded on the stair.

If they are gone it means a few days more
Are left, or they would wait. Joel would wait
Down by the dark old clock that told me late
That night from Boston. "Evans walked me home;
We sat together in the train by chance."
But not a word; only his burning glance.
"Why do you stand like that? What if I come
An hour or so after the time I said?
The house all dark, I thought you'd gone to bed."
But still that gaze, not anger, indignation,
Nor anything so easy, but a look
As fixed as when he stared upon his book.
No matter if my tale was false or true,
I was a woodcut figure on the page,
On trial for a nameless sin. Then rage
Took him like fire where lightning dives. I knew
That he could kill me then, but what he did
Was wrench me up the stairs, onto the bed.

The night of Joel's death I slept alone
In this same room. A neighbor said she'd stay,
Thinking the dead man lying down below
Might keep the living from rest. She told me so:
"Those hours before the dawn can lie like stone
Upon the heart—I've lain awake—I know."
At last I had to take the only way,
And said, "The nights he was alive and walking
From room to room and hearing spirits talking,
What sleep I had was likelier to be broken."
Her face was shocked but I was glad I'd spoken.
"Well, if you feel so—" She would tell the tale
Next morning, but at last I was alone
In an existence finally my own.

And yet I knew that Evans would find reason
Why we were not our own, nor had our will
Unhindered; that disturbance of a season
So long removed was something he would kill
Yet, if he had not killed it. When I stood

Beside the churchyard fence and felt his glance
Reluctantly compelling mine, the blood
Soared to my face, the tombstones seemed to dance
Dizzily, till I turned. The eyes I met
Accused as they implored me to forget,
As if my shape had risen to destroy
Salvation's rampart with a hope of joy.
My lips betrayed their *Why?* but then his face
Turned from me, and I saw him leave the place.
Now Joel and Evans are neighbors, down beneath.

I wonder what we're bound to after death?
I wonder what's exacted of the dead,
How many debts of conscience still are good?
Not Evans or his Bible ever said
That spirit must complete what flesh and blood
Contracted in their term. What creditors
Will wait and knock for us at marble doors?

I'd like to know which stays when life is past:
The marriage kept in fear, the love deferred,
The footstep waited for and never heard,
The pressure of five fingers round the wrist
Stopping its beat with pain, the mouth unkissed,
The dream whose waking startles into sight
A figure mumbling by the bed at night,
The hopeless promise of eternal life—
Take now your Scripture, Evans, if you will,
And see how flimsily the pages spill
From spines reduced to dust. What have they said
Of us, to what will they pronounce me wife?
My debt is paid: the rest is on your head.

From

*Snapshots of a
Daughter-in-Law*

1963

From Morning-Glory to Petersburg

(*The World Book,* 1928)

"Organized knowledge in story and picture"
    confronts through dusty glass
    an eye grown dubious.
I can recall when knowledge still was pure,
    not contradictory, pleasurable
    as cutting out a paper doll.
You opened up a book and there it was:
    everything just as promised, from
    Kurdistan to Mormons, Gum
Arabic to Kumquat, neither more nor less.
    Facts could be kept separate
    by a convention; that was what
made childhood possible. Now knowledge finds me out;
    in all its risible untidiness
    it traces me to each address,
dragging in things I never thought about.
    I don't invite what facts can be
    held at arm's length; a family
of jeering irresponsibles always
    comes along gypsy-style
    and there you have them all
forever on your hands. It never pays.
    If I could still extrapolate
    the morning-glory on the gate
from Petersburg in history—but it's too late.

1954

Rural Reflections

This is the grass your feet are planted on.
You paint it orange or you sing it green,
    But you have never found
A way to make the grass mean what you mean.

A cloud can be whatever you intend:
Ostrich or leaning tower or staring eye.
    But you have never found
A cloud sufficient to express the sky.

Get out there with your splendid expertise;
Raymond who cuts the meadow does no less.
    Inhuman nature says:
Inhuman patience is the true success.

Human impatience trips you as you run;
    Stand still and you must lie.
It is the grass that cuts the mower down;
It is the cloud that swallows up the sky.

1956

The Knight

A knight rides into the noon,
and his helmet points to the sun,
and a thousand splintered suns
are the gaiety of his mail.
The soles of his feet glitter
and his palms flash in reply,
and under his crackling banner
he rides like a ship in sail.

●

A knight rides into the noon,
and only his eye is living,
a lump of bitter jelly
set in a metal mask,
betraying rags and tatters
that cling to the flesh beneath
and wear his nerves to ribbons
under the radiant casque.

Who will unhorse this rider
and free him from between
the walls of iron, the emblems
crushing his chest with their weight?
Will they defeat him gently,
or leave him hurled on the green,
his rags and wounds still hidden
under the great breastplate?

1957

The Loser

*A man thinks of the woman he
once loved: first, after her wedding,
and then nearly a decade later.*

1.

I kissed you, bride and lost, and went
home from that bourgeois sacrament,
your cheek still tasting cold upon
my lips that gave you benison
with all the swagger that they knew—
as losers somehow learn to do.

●

Your wedding made my eyes ache; soon
the world would be worse off for one
more golden apple dropped to ground
without the least protesting sound,
and you would windfall lie, and we
forget your shimmer on the tree.

Beauty is always wasted: if
not Mignon's song sung to the deaf,
at all events to the unmoved.
A face like yours cannot be loved
long or seriously enough.
Almost, we seem to hold it off.

2.

Well, you are tougher than I thought.
Now when the wash with ice hangs taut
this morning of St. Valentine,
I see you strip the squeaking line,
your body weighed against the load,
and all my groans can do no good.

Because you still are beautiful,
Though squared and stiffened by the pull
of what nine windy years have done.
You have three daughters, lost a son.
I see all your intelligence
flung into that unwearied stance.

My envy is of no avail.
I turn my head and wish him well
who chafed your beauty into use
and lives forever in a house
lit by the friction of your mind.
You stagger in against the wind.

1958

Snapshots of a Daughter-in-Law

1.

You, once a belle in Shreveport,
with henna-colored hair, skin like a peachbud,
still have your dresses copied from that time,
and play a Chopin prelude
called by Cortot: *"Delicious recollections*
float like perfume through the memory."

Your mind now, moldering like wedding-cake,
heavy with useless experience, rich
with suspicion, rumor, fantasy,
crumbling to pieces under the knife-edge
of mere fact. In the prime of your life.

Nervy, glowering, your daughter
wipes the teaspoons, grows another way.

2.

Banging the coffee-pot into the sink
she hears the angels chiding, and looks out
past the raked gardens to the sloppy sky.
Only a week since They said: *Have no patience.*

The next time it was: *Be insatiable.*
Then: *Save yourself; others you cannot save.*
Sometimes she's let the tapstream scald her arm,
a match burn to her thumbnail,

or held her hand above the kettle's snout
right in the woolly steam. They are probably angels,
since nothing hurts her anymore, except
each morning's grit blowing into her eyes.

•

3.

A thinking woman sleeps with monsters.
The beak that grips her, she becomes. And Nature,
that sprung-lidded, still commodious
steamer-trunk of *tempora* and *mores*
gets stuffed with it all: the mildewed orange-flowers,
the female pills, the terrible breasts
of Boadicea beneath flat foxes' heads and orchids.

Two handsome women, gripped in argument,
each proud, acute, subtle, I hear scream
across the cut glass and majolica
like Furies cornered from their prey:
The argument *ad feminam*, all the old knives
that have rusted in my back, I drive in yours,
ma semblable, ma soeur!

4.

Knowing themselves too well in one another:
their gifts no pure fruition, but a thorn,
the prick filed sharp against a hint of scorn . . .
Reading while waiting
for the iron to heat,
writing, *My Life had stood—a Loaded Gun—*
in that Amherst pantry while the jellies boil and scum,
or, more often,
iron-eyed and beaked and purposed as a bird,
dusting everything on the whatnot every day of life.

5.

Dulce ridens, dulce loquens,
she shaves her legs until they gleam
like petrified mammoth-tusk.

6.

When to her lute Corinna sings
neither words nor music are her own;

only the long hair dipping
over her cheek, only the song
of silk against her knees
and these
adjusted in reflections of an eye.

Poised, trembling and unsatisfied, before
an unlocked door, that cage of cages,
tell us, you bird, you tragical machine—
is this *fertilisante douleur?* Pinned down
by love, for you the only natural action,
are you edged more keen
to prise the secrets of the vault? has Nature shown
her household books to you, daughter-in-law,
that her sons never saw?

7.

*"To have in this uncertain world some stay
which cannot be undermined, is
of the utmost consequence."*
                                    Thus wrote
a woman, partly brave and partly good,
who fought with what she partly understood.
Few men about her would or could do more,
hence she was labeled harpy, shrew and whore.

8.

"You all die at fifteen," said Diderot,
and turn part legend, part convention.
Still, eyes inaccurately dream
behind closed windows blankening with steam.
Deliciously, all that we might have been,
all that we were—fire, tears,
wit, taste, martyred ambition—
stirs like the memory of refused adultery
the drained and flagging bosom of our middle years.

•

9.

Not that it is done well, but
that it is done at all? Yes, think
of the odds! or shrug them off forever.
This luxury of the precocious child,
Time's precious chronic invalid,—
would we, darlings, resign it if we could?
Our blight has been our sinecure:
mere talent was enough for us—
glitter in fragments and rough drafts.

Sigh no more, ladies.
                    Time is male
and in his cups drinks to the fair.
Bemused by gallantry, we hear
our mediocrities over-praised,
indolence read as abnegation,
slattern thought styled intuition,
every lapse forgiven, our crime
only to cast too bold a shadow
or smash the mold straight off.

For that, solitary confinement,
tear gas, attrition shelling.
Few applicants for that honor.

10.
                              Well,
she's long about her coming, who must be
more merciless to herself than history.
Her mind full to the wind, I see her plunge
breasted and glancing through the currents,
taking the light upon her
at least as beautiful as any boy
or helicopter,
                    poised, still coming,
her fine blades making the air wince

but her cargo
no promise then:
delivered
palpable
ours.

1958–1960

Antinoüs: The Diaries

Autumn torture. The old signs
smeared on the pavement, sopping leaves
rubbed into the landscape as unguent on a bruise,
brought indoors, even, as they bring flowers, enormous,
with the colors of the body's secret parts.
All this. And then, evenings, needing to be out,
walking fast, fighting the fire
that must die, light that sets my teeth on edge with joy,
till on the black embankment
I'm a cart stopped in the ruts of time.

Then at some house the rumor of truth and beauty
saturates a room like lilac-water
in the steam of a bath, fires snap, heads are high,
gold hair at napes of necks, gold in glasses,
gold in the throat, poetry of furs and manners.
Why do I shiver then? Haven't I seen,
over and over, before the end of an evening,
the three opened coffins carried in and left in a corner?
Haven't I watched as somebody cracked his shin
on one of them, winced and hopped and limped
laughing to lay his hand on a beautiful arm
striated with hairs of gold, like an almond-shell?

●

The old, needless story. For if I'm here
it is by choice and when at last
I smell my own rising nausea, feel the air
tighten around my stomach like a surgical bandage,
I can't pretend surprise. What is it I so miscarry?
If what I spew on the tiles at last,
helpless, disgraced, alone,
is in part what I've swallowed from glasses, eyes,
motions of hands, opening and closing mouths,
isn't it also dead gobbets of myself,
abortive, murdered, or never willed?

1959

Merely to Know

1.

Wedged in by earthworks
thrown up by snouters before me,
I kick and snuffle, breathing in
cobwebs of beetle-cuirass:
vainglory of polished green,
infallible pincer, resonant nerve,
a thickening on the air now,
confusion to my lungs, no more.
My predecessors blind me—
their zeal exhausted among roots and tunnels,
they gasped and looked up once or twice
into the beechtree's nightblack glitter.

2.

Let me take you by the hair
and drag you backward to the light,
there spongelike press my gaze
patiently upon your eyes,

hold like a photographic plate
against you my enormous question.
What if you cringe, what if you weep?
Suffer this and you need suffer
nothing more. I'll give you back
yourself at last to the last part.
I take nothing, only look.
Change nothing. Have no need to change.
Merely to know and let you go.

1959

3.

Spirit like water
molded by unseen stone
and sandbar, pleats and funnels
according to its own
submerged necessity—
to the indolent eye
pure willfulness, to the stray
pine-needle boiling
in that cascade-bent pool
a random fury: Law,
if that's what's wanted, lies
asking to be read
in the dried brook-bed.

1961

Juvenilia

Your Ibsen volumes, violet-spined,
each flaking its gold arabesque . . .
Again I sit, under duress, hands washed,
at your inkstained oaken desk,

by the goose-neck lamp in the tropic of your books,
stabbing the blotting-pad, doodling loop upon loop,
peering one-eyed in the dusty reflecting mirror
of your student microscope,
craning my neck to spell above me

A DOLL'S HOUSE   LITTLE EYOLF
    WHEN WE DEAD AWAKEN

Unspeakable fairy tales ebb like blood through my head
as I dip the pen and for aunts, for admiring friends,
for you above all to read,
copy my praised and sedulous lines.

Behind the two of us, thirsty spines
quiver in semi-shadow, huge leaves uncurl and thicken.

1960

A Woman Mourned
by Daughters

Now, not a tear begun,
we sit here in your kitchen,
spent, you see, already.
You are swollen till you strain
this house and the whole sky.
You, whom we so often
succeeded in ignoring!
You are puffed up in death
like a corpse pulled from the sea;
we groan beneath your weight.
And yet you were a leaf,
a straw blown on the bed,
you had long since become
crisp as a dead insect.

What is it, if not you,
that settles on us now
like satin you pulled down
over our bridal heads?
What rises in our throats
like food you prodded in?
Nothing could be enough.
You breathe upon us now
through solid assertions
of yourself: teaspoons, goblets,
seas of carpet, a forest
of old plants to be watered,
an old man in an adjoining
room to be touched and fed.
And all this universe
dares us to lay a finger
anywhere, save exactly
as you would wish it done.

1960

The Afterwake

Nursing your nerves
to rest, I've roused my own; well,
now for a few bad hours!
Sleep sees you behind closed doors.
Alone, I slump in his front parlor.
You're safe inside. Good. But I'm
like a midwife who at dawn
has all in order: bloodstains
washed up, teapot on the stove,
and starts her five miles home
walking, the birthyell still
exploding in her head.

●

Yes, I'm with her now: here's
the streaked, livid road
edged with shut houses
breathing night out and in.
Legs tight with fatigue,
we move under morning's coal-blue star,
colossal as this load
of unexpired purpose, which drains
slowly, till scissors of cockcrow snip the air.

1961

A Marriage in the 'Sixties

As solid-seeming as antiquity,
you frown above
the *New York Sunday Times*
where Castro, like a walk-on out of *Carmen,*
mutters into a bearded henchman's ear.

They say the second's getting shorter—
I knew it in my bones—
and pieces of the universe are missing.
I feel the gears of this late afternoon
slip, cog by cog, even as I read.
"I'm old," we both complain,
half-laughing, oftener now.

Time serves you well. That face—
part Roman emperor, part Raimu—
nothing this side of Absence can undo.
Bliss, revulsion, your rare angers can
only carry through what's well begun.

•

When
I read your letters long ago
in that half-defunct
hotel in Magdalen Street
every word primed my nerves.
A geographical misery
composed of oceans, fogbound planes
and misdelivered cablegrams
lay round me, a Nova Zembla
only your live breath could unfreeze.
Today we stalk
in the raging desert of our thought
whose single drop of mercy is
each knows the other there.
Two strangers, thrust for life upon a rock,
may have at last the perfect hour of talk
that language aches for; still—
two minds, two messages.

Your brows knit into flourishes. Some piece
of mere time has you tangled there.
Some mote of history has flown into your eye.
Will nothing ever be the same,
even our quarrels take a different key,
our dreams exhume new metaphors?
The world breathes underneath our bed.
Don't look. We're at each other's mercy too.

Dear fellow-particle, electric dust
I'm blown with—ancestor
to what euphoric cluster—
see how particularity dissolves
in all that hints of chaos. Let one finger
hover toward you from There
and see this furious grain
suspend its dance to hang
beside you like your twin.

1961

Attention

The ice age is here.
I sit burning cigarettes,
burning my brain.
A micro-Tibet,
deadly, frivolous, complete,
blinds the four panes.
Veils of dumb air
unwind like bandages
from my lips
half-parted, steady as the mouths
of antique statues.

1961

Artificial Intelligence

Over the chessboard now,
Your Artificiality concludes
a final check; rests; broods—
        no—sorts and stacks a file of memories,
while I
concede the victory, bow,
and slouch among my free associations.

You never had a mother,
let's say? no digital Gertrude
whom you'd as lief have seen
Kingless? So your White Queen
was just an "operator."
(My Red had incandescence,
ire, aura, flare,
and trapped me several moments in her stare.)

•

I'm sulking, clearly, in the great tradition
of human waste. Why not
dump the whole reeking snarl
and let you solve me once for all?
(*Parameter:* a black-faced Luddite
itching for ecstasies of sabotage.)

Still, when
they make you write your poems, later on,
who'd envy you, force-fed
on all those variorum
editions of our primitive endeavors,
those frozen pemmican language-rations
they'll cram you with? denied
our luxury of nausea, you
forget nothing, have no dreams.

1961

Sisters

Can I easily say,
I know you of course now,
no longer the fellow-victim,
reader of my diaries, heir
to my outgrown dresses,
ear for my poems and invectives?
Do I know you better
than that blue-eyed stranger
self-absorbed as myself
raptly knitting or sleeping
through a thirdclass winter journey?
Face to face all night
her dreams and whimpers
tangled with mine,
sleeping but not asleep

behind the engine drilling
into dark Germany,
her eyes, mouth, head
reconstructed by dawn
as we nodded farewell.
Her I should recognize
years later, anywhere.

1961

Peeling Onions

Only to have a grief
equal to all these tears!

There's not a sob in my chest.
Dry-hearted as Peer Gynt
I pare away, no hero,
merely a cook.

Crying was labor, once
when I'd good cause.
Walking, I felt my eyes like wounds
raw in my head,
so postal-clerks, I thought, must stare.
A dog's look, a cat's, burnt to my brain—
yet all that stayed
stuffed in my lungs like smog.

These old tears in the chopping-bowl.

1961

The Roofwalker

—for Denise Levertov

Over the half-finished houses
night comes. The builders
stand on the roof. It is
quiet after the hammers,
the pulleys hang slack.
Giants, the roofwalkers,
on a listing deck, the wave
of darkness about to break
on their heads. The sky
is a torn sail where figures
pass magnified, shadows
on a burning deck.

I feel like them up there:
exposed, larger than life,
and due to break my neck.

Was it worth while to lay—
with infinite exertion—
a roof I can't live under?
—All those blueprints,
closings of gaps,
measurings, calculations?
A life I didn't choose
chose me: even
my tools are the wrong ones
for what I have to do.
I'm naked, ignorant,
a naked man fleeing
across the roofs
who could with a shade of difference
be sitting in the lamplight

against the cream wallpaper
reading—not with indifference—
about a naked man
fleeing across the roofs.

1961

Ghost of a Chance

You see a man
trying to think.

You want to say
to everything:
Keep off! Give him room!
But you only watch,
terrified
the old consolations
will get him at last
like a fish
half-dead from flopping
and almost crawling
across the shingle,
almost breathing
the raw, agonizing
air
till a wave
pulls it back blind into the triumphant
sea.

1962

Novella

Two people in a room, speaking harshly.
One gets up, goes out to walk.
(That is the man.)
The other goes into the next room
and washes the dishes, cracking one.
(That is the woman.)
It gets dark outside.
The children quarrel in the attic.
She has no blood left in her heart.
The man comes back to a dark house.
The only light is in the attic.
He has forgotten his key.
He rings at his own door
and hears sobbing on the stairs.
The lights go on in the house.
The door closes behind him.
Outside, separate as minds,
the stars too come alight.

1962

Prospective Immigrants
Please Note

Either you will
go through this door
or you will not go through.

If you go through
there is always the risk
of remembering your name.

•

Things look at you doubly
and you must look back
and let them happen.

If you do not go through
it is possible
to live worthily

to maintain your attitudes
to hold your position
to die bravely

but much will blind you,
much will evade you,
at what cost who knows?

The door itself
makes no promises.
It is only a door.

1962

From

Necessities of Life

1966

Necessities of Life

Piece by piece I seem
to re-enter the world: I first began

a small, fixed dot, still see
that old myself, a dark-blue thumbtack

pushed into the scene,
a hard little head protruding

from the pointillist's buzz and bloom.
After a time the dot

begins to ooze. Certain heats
melt it.
       Now I was hurriedly

blurring into ranges
of burnt red, burning green,

whole biographies swam up and
swallowed me like Jonah.

Jonah! I was Wittgenstein,
Mary Wollstonecraft, the soul

of Louis Jouvet, dead
in a blown-up photograph.

Till, wolfed almost to shreds,
I learned to make myself

unappetizing. Scaly as a dry bulb
thrown into a cellar

•   55

I used myself, let nothing use me.
Like being on a private dole,

sometimes more like kneading bricks in Egypt.
What life was there, was mine,

now and again to lay
one hand on a warm brick

and touch the sun's ghost
with economical joy,

now and again to name
over the bare necessities.

So much for those days. Soon
practice may make me middling-perfect, I'll

dare inhabit the world
trenchant in motion as an eel, solid

as a cabbage-head. I have invitations:
a curl of mist steams upward

from a field, visible as my breath,
houses along a road stand waiting

like old women knitting, breathless
to tell their tales.

1962

In the Woods

"Difficult ordinary happiness,"
no one nowadays believes in you.

I shift, full-length on the blanket,
to fix the sun precisely

behind the pine-tree's crest
so light spreads through the needles
alive as water just
where a snake has surfaced,

unreal as water in green crystal.
Bad news is always arriving.
"We're hiders, hiding from something bad,"
sings the little boy.

Writing these words in the woods,
I feel like a traitor to my friends,
even to my enemies.
The common lot's to die

a stranger's death and lie
rouged in the coffin, in a dress
chosen by the funeral director.
Perhaps that's why we never

see clocks on public buildings any more.
A fact no architect will mention.
We're hiders, hiding from something bad
most of the time.

Yet, and outrageously, something good
finds us, found me this morning
lying on a dusty blanket
among the burnt-out Indian pipes

and bursting-open lady's-slippers.
My soul, my helicopter, whirred
distantly, by habit, over
the old pond with the half-drowned boat

toward which it always veers
for consolation: ego's Arcady:

leaving the body stuck
like a leaf against a screen.—

Happiness! how many times
I've stranded on that word,
at the edge of that pond; seen
as if through tears, the dragon-fly—

only to find it all
going differently for once
this time: my soul wheeled back
and burst into my body.

Found! Ready or not.
If I move now, the sun
naked between the trees
will melt me as I lie.

1963

The Corpse-Plant

> *How can an obedient man, or a sick man,*
> *dare to write poems?*
> *—Walt Whitman*

A milk-glass bowl hanging by three chains
from the discolored ceiling
is beautiful tonight. On the floor, leaves, crayons,
innocent dust foregather.

Neither obedient nor sick, I turn my head,
feeling the weight of a thick gold ring
in either lobe. I see the corpse-plants
 clustered in a hobnailed tumbler

at my elbow, white as death, I'd say,
if I'd ever seen death;
whiter than life
next to my summer-stained hand.

Is it in the sun that truth begins?
Lying under that battering light
the first few hours of summer
I felt scraped clean, washed down

to ignorance. The gold in my ears,
souvenir of a shrewd old city,
might have been wearing thin as wires
found in the bones of a woman's head

miraculously kept in its essentials
in some hot cradle-tomb of time.
I felt my body slipping through
the fingers of its mind.

Later, I slid on wet rocks,
threw my shoes across a brook,
waded on algae-furred stones
to join them. That day I found

the corpse-plants, growing like
shadows on a negative
in the chill of fern and lichen-rust.
That day for the first time

I gave them their deathly names—
or did they name themselves?—
not "Indian pipes" as once
we children knew them.

Tonight, I think of winter,
winters of mind, of flesh,
sickness of the rot-smell of leaves
turned silt-black, heavy as tarpaulin,

●

obedience of the elevator cage
lowering itself, crank by crank
into the mine-pit,
forced labor forcibly renewed—

but the horror is dimmed:
like the negative of one
intolerable photograph
it barely sorts itself out

under the radiance of the milk-glass shade.
Only death's insect whiteness
crooks its neck in a tumbler
where I placed its sign by choice.

1963

The Trees

The trees inside are moving out into the forest,
the forest that was empty all these days
where no bird could sit
no insect hide
no sun bury its feet in shadow
the forest that was empty all these nights
will be full of trees by morning.

All night the roots work
to disengage themselves from the cracks
in the veranda floor.
The leaves strain toward the glass
small twigs stiff with exertion
long-cramped boughs shuffling under the roof
like newly discharged patients
half-dazed, moving
to the clinic doors.

•

I sit inside, doors open to the veranda
writing long letters
in which I scarcely mention the departure
of the forest from the house.
The night is fresh, the whole moon shines
in a sky still open
the smell of leaves and lichen
still reaches like a voice into the rooms.
My head is full of whispers
which tomorrow will be silent.

Listen. The glass is breaking.
The trees are stumbling forward
into the night. Winds rush to meet them.
The moon is broken like a mirror,
its pieces flash now in the crown
of the tallest oak.

1963

Like This Together

—for A.H.C.

1.

Wind rocks the car.
We sit parked by the river,
silence between our teeth.
Birds scatter across islands
of broken ice. Another time
I'd have said: "Canada geese,"
knowing you love them.
A year, ten years from now
I'll remember this—
this sitting like drugged birds

in a glass case—
not why, only that we
were here like this together.

2.

They're tearing down, tearing up
this city, block by block.
Rooms cut in half
hang like flayed carcasses,
their old roses in rags,
famous streets have forgotten
where they were going. Only
a fact could be so dreamlike.
They're tearing down the houses
we met and lived in,
soon our two bodies will be all
left standing from that era.

3.

We have, as they say,
certain things in common.
I mean: a view
from a bathroom window
over slate to stiff pigeons
huddled every morning; the way
water tastes from our tap,
which you marvel at, letting
it splash into the glass.
Because of you I notice
the taste of water,
a luxury I might
otherwise have missed.

4.

Our words misunderstand us.
Sometimes at night
you are my mother:

old detailed griefs
twitch at my dreams, and I
crawl against you, fighting
for shelter, making you
my cave. Sometimes
you're the wave of birth
that drowns me in my first
nightmare. I suck the air.
Miscarried knowledge twists us
like hot sheets thrown askew.

5.

Dead winter doesn't die,
it wears away, a piece of carrion
picked clean at last,
rained away or burnt dry.
Our desiring does this,
make no mistake, I'm speaking
of fact: through mere indifference
we could prevent it.
Only our fierce attention
gets hyacinths out of those
hard cerebral lumps,
unwraps the wet buds down
the whole length of a stem.

1963

Open-Air Museum

Ailanthus, goldenrod, scrapiron, what makes you flower?
What burns in the dump today?

Thick flames in a grey field, tended
by two men: one derelict ghost,

one clearly apter at nursing destruction,
two priests in a grey field, tending the flames
of stripped-off rockwool, split
mattresses, a caved-in chickenhouse,
mad Lou's last stack of paintings, each a perfect black lozenge

seen from a train, stopped
as by design, to bring us
face to face with the flag of our true country:
violet-yellow, black-violet,
its heart sucked by slow fire
O my America
this then was your desire?

but you cannot burn fast enough:
in the photograph the white
skirts of the Harlem bride
are lashed by blown scraps, tabloid sheets,
her beauty a scrap of flickering light
licked by a greater darkness

This then was your desire!
those trucked-off bad dreams
outside the city limits
crawl back in search of you, eyes
missing, skins missing, intenser in decay
the carriage that wheeled the defective baby
rolls up on three wheels
and the baby is still inside,
you cannot burn fast enough
Blue sparks of the chicory flower
flash from embers of the dump
inside the rose-rust carcass of a slaughtered Chevrolet
crouches the young ailanthus

and the two guardians go raking the sacred field, raking
slowly, to what endless end

Cry of truth among so many lies
at your heart burns on
a languid fire

1964

Two Songs

1.

Sex, as they harshly call it,
I fell into this morning
at ten o'clock, a drizzling hour
of traffic and wet newspapers.
I thought of him who yesterday
clearly didn't
turn me to a hot field
ready for plowing,
and longing for that young man
piercéd me to the roots
bathing every vein, etc.
All day he appears to me
touchingly desirable,
a prize one could wreck one's peace for.
I'd call it love if love
didn't take so many years
but lust too is a jewel
a sweet flower and what
pure happiness to know
all our high-toned questions
breed in a lively animal.

2.

That "old last act"!
And yet sometimes
all seems post coitum triste

and I a mere bystander.
Somebody else is going off,
getting shot to the moon.
Or, a moon-race!
Split seconds after
my opposite number lands
I make it—
we lie fainting together
at a crater-edge
heavy as mercury in our moonsuits
till he speaks—
in a different language
yet one I've picked up
through cultural exchanges . . .
we murmur the first moonwords:
Spasibo. Thanks. O.K.

1964

The Parting: I

The ocean twanging away there
and the islands like scattered laundry—

You can feel so free, so free,
standing on the headland

where the wild rose never stands still,
the petals blown off

before they fall
and the chicory nodding

blue, blue, in the all-day wind.
Barbed wire, dead at your feet,

•

is a kind of dune-vine,
the only one without movement.

Every knot is a knife
where two strands tangle to rust.

1963

Night-Pieces: For a Child

1. *The Crib*

You sleeping I bend to cover.
Your eyelids work. I see
your dream, cloudy as a negative,
swimming underneath.
You blurt a cry. Your eyes
spring open, still filmed in dream.
Wider, they fix me—
—death's head, sphinx, medusa?
You scream.
Tears lick my cheeks, my knees
droop at your fear.
Mother I no more am,
but woman, and nightmare.

2. *Her Waking*

Tonight I jerk astart in a dark
hourless as Hiroshima,
almost hearing you breathe
in a cot three doors away.

You still breathe, yes—
and my dream with its gift of knives,
its murderous hider and seeker,
ebbs away, recoils

●

back into the egg of dreams,
the vanishing point of mind.
All gone.

But you and I—
swaddled in a dumb dark
old as sickheartedness,
modern as pure annihilation—

we drift in ignorance.
If I could hear you now
mutter some gentle animal sound!
If milk flowed from my breast again. . . .

1964

After Dark

1.

You are falling asleep and I sit looking at you
old tree of life
old man whose death I wanted
I can't stir you up now.

Faintly a phonograph needle
whirs round in the last groove
eating my heart to dust.
That terrible record! how it played

down years, wherever I was
in foreign languages even
over and over, *I know you better
than you know yourself   I know*

*you better than you know
yourself   I know*

•

you   until, self-maimed,
I limped off, torn at the roots,

stopped singing a whole year,
got a new body, new breath,
got children, croaked for words,
forgot to listen

or read your *mene tekel* fading on the wall,
woke up one morning
and knew myself your daughter.
Blood is a sacred poison.

Now, unasked, you give ground.
We only want to stifle
what's stifling us already.
Alive now, root to crown, I'd give

—oh,—something—not to know
our struggles now are ended.
I seem to hold you, cupped
in my hands, and disappearing.

When your memory fails—
no more to scourge my inconsistencies—
the sashcords of the world fly loose.
A window crashes

suddenly down. I go to the woodbox
and take a stick of kindling
to prop the sash again.
I grow protective toward the world.

2.

Now let's away from prison—
Underground seizures!
I used to huddle in the grave
I'd dug for you and bite

•

my tongue for fear it would babble
—*Darling*—
I thought they'd find me there
someday, sitting upright, shrunken,

my hair like roots and in my lap
a mess of broken pottery—
wasted libation—
and you embalmed beside me.

No, let's away. Even now
there's a walk between doomed elms
(whose like we shall not see much longer)
and something—grass and water—

an old dream-photograph.
I'll sit with you there and tease you
for wisdom, if you like,
waiting till the blunt barge

bumps along the shore.
Poppies burn in the twilight
like smudge pots.
I think you hardly see me

but—this is the dream now—
your fears blow out,
off, over the water.
At the last, your hand feels steady.

1964

"I Am in Danger—Sir—"

"Half-cracked" to Higginson, living,
—afterward famous in garbled versions,

your hoard of dazzling scraps a battlefield,
now your old snood

mothballed at Harvard
and you in your variorum monument
equivocal to the end—
who are you?

Gardening the day-lily,
wiping the wine-glass stems,
your thought pulsed on behind
a forehead battered paper-thin,

you, woman, masculine
in single-mindedness,
for whom the word was more
than a symptom—

a condition of being.
Till the air buzzing with spoiled language
sang in your ears
of Perjury

and in your half-cracked way you chose
silence for entertainment,
chose to have it out at last
on your own premises.

1964

Mourning Picture

The picture was painted by Edwin Romanzo Elmer
(1850–1923) as a memorial to his daughter Effie.
In the poem, it is the dead girl who speaks.

They have carried the mahogany chair and the cane rocker
out under the lilac bush,
and my father and mother darkly sit there, in black clothes.
Our clapboard house stands fast on its hill,
my doll lies in her wicker pram
gazing at western Massachusetts.
This was our world.
I could remake each shaft of grass
feeling its rasp on my fingers,
draw out the map of every lilac leaf
or the net of veins on my father's
grief-tranced hand.

Out of my head, half-bursting,
still filling, the dream condenses—
shadows, crystals, ceilings, meadows, globes of dew.
Under the dull green of the lilacs, out in the light
carving each spoke of the pram, the turned porch-pillars,
under high early-summer clouds,
I am Effie, visible and invisible,
remembering and remembered.

They will move from the house,
give the toys and pets away.
Mute and rigid with loss my mother
will ride the train to Baptist Corner,
the silk-spool will run bare.
I tell you, the thread that bound us lies
faint as a web in the dew.
Should I make you, world, again,

could I give back the leaf its skeleton, the air
its early-summer cloud, the house
its noonday presence, shadowless,
and leave *this* out? I am Effie, you were my dream.

1965

Halfway

—in memory: M.G.J.

In the field the air writhes, a heat-pocket.
Masses of birds revolve, blades
of a harvester.
The sky is getting milkily white,
a sac of light is ready to burst open.

Time of hailstones and rainbow.
My life flows North. At last I understand.
A young girl, thought sleeping, is certified dead.
A tray of expensive waxen fruit,
she lies arranged on the spare-room coverlid.

To sit by the fire is to become another woman,
red hair charring to grey,
green eyes grappling with the printed page,
voice flailing, flailing the uncomprehending.
My days lie open, listening, grandmother.

1965

The Knot

In the heart of the queen anne's lace, a knot of blood.
For years I never saw it,

years of metallic vision,
spears glancing off a bright eyeball,

suns off a Swiss lake.
A foaming meadow; the Milky Way;

and there, all along, the tiny dark-red spider
sitting in the whiteness of the bridal web,

waiting to plunge his crimson knifepoint
into the white apparencies.

Little wonder the eye, healing, sees
for a long time through a mist of blood.

1965

Moth Hour

Space mildews at our touch.
The leaves of the poplar, slowly moving—
aren't they moth-white, there in the moonbeams?
A million insects die every twilight,
no one even finds their corpses.
Death, slowly moving among the bleached clouds,
knows us better than we know ourselves.

•

I am gliding backward away from those who knew me
as the moon grows thinner and finally shuts its lantern.
I can be replaced a thousand times,
a box containing death.
When you put out your hand to touch me
you are already reaching toward an empty space.

1965

Focus

—for Bert Dreyfus

Obscurity has its tale to tell.
Like the figure on the studio-bed in the corner,

out of range, smoking, watching and waiting.
Sun pours through the skylight onto the worktable

making of a jar of pencils, a typewriter keyboard
more than they were. Veridical light . . .

Earth budges. Now an empty coffee-cup,
a whetstone, a handkerchief, take on

their sacramental clarity, fixed by the wand
of light as the thinker thinks to fix them in the mind.

O secret in the core of the whetstone, in the five
pencils splayed out like fingers of a hand!

The mind's passion is all for singling out.
Obscurity has another tale to tell.

1965

Face to Face

Never to be lonely like that—
the Early American figure on the beach
in black coat and knee-breeches
scanning the didactic storm in privacy,

never to hear the prairie wolves
in their lunar hilarity
circling one's little all, one's claim
to be Law and Prophets

for all that lawlessness,
never to whet the appetite
weeks early, for a face, a hand
longed-for and dreaded—

How people used to meet!
starved, intense, the old
Christmas gifts saved up till spring,
and the old plain words,

and each with his God-given secret,
spelled out through months of snow and silence,
burning under the bleached scalp; behind dry lips
a loaded gun.

1965

From

Leaflets

1969

Orion

Far back when I went zig-zagging
through tamarack pastures
you were my genius, you
my cast-iron Viking, my helmed
lion-heart king in prison.
Years later now you're young

my fierce half-brother, staring
down from that simplified west
your breast open, your belt dragged down
by an oldfashioned thing, a sword
the last bravado you won't give over
though it weighs you down as you stride

and the stars in it are dim
and maybe have stopped burning.
But you burn, and I know it;
as I throw back my head to take you in
an old transfusion happens again:
divine astronomy is nothing to it.

Indoors I bruise and blunder,
break faith, leave ill enough
alone, a dead child born in the dark.
Night cracks up over the chimney,
pieces of time, frozen geodes
come showering down in the grate.

A man reaches behind my eyes
and finds them empty
a woman's head turns away
from my head in the mirror
children are dying my death
and eating crumbs of my life.

Pity is not your forte.
Calmly you ache up there
pinned aloft in your crow's nest,
my speechless pirate!
You take it all for granted
and when I look you back

it's with a starlike eye
shooting its cold and egotistical spear
where it can do least damage.
Breathe deep! No hurt, no pardon
out here in the cold with you
you with your back to the wall.

1965

Holding Out

The hunters' shack will do,
abandoned, untended, unmended
in its cul-de-sac of alders.
Inside, who knows what
hovel-keeping essentials—
a grey saucepan, a broom, a clock
stopped at last autumn's last hour—
all or any, what matter.

The point is, it's a shelter,
a place more in- than outside.
From that we could begin.
And the wind is surely rising,
snow is in the alders.
Maybe the stovepipe is sound,
maybe the smoke will do us in
at first—no matter.

●

Late afternoons the ice
squeaks underfoot like mica,
and when the sun drops red and moon-
faced back of the gun-colored firs,
the best intentions are none too good.
Then we have to make a go of it
in the smoke with the dark outside
and our love in our boots at first—
no matter.

1965

In the Evening

Three hours chain-smoking words
and you move on. We stand in the porch,
two archaic figures: a woman and a man.

The old masters, the old sources,
haven't a clue what we're about,
shivering here in the half-dark 'sixties.

Our minds hover in a famous impasse
and cling together. Your hand
grips mine like a railing on an icy night.

The wall of the house is bleeding. Firethorn!
The moon, cracked every-which-way,
pushes steadily on.

1966

The Demon Lover

Fatigue, regrets. The lights
go out in the parking lot
two by two. Snow blindness
settles over the suburb.
Desire. Desire. The nebula
opens in space, unseen,
your heart utters its great beats
in solitude. A new
era is coming in.
Gauche as we are, it seems
we have to play our part.

A plaid dress, silk scarf,
and eyes that go on stinging.
Woman, stand off. The air
glistens like silk.
She's gone. In her place stands
a schoolgirl, morning light,
the half-grown bones
of innocence. Is she
your daughter or your muse,
this tree of blondness
grown up in a field of thorns?

Something piercing and marred.
Take note. Look back. When quick
the whole northeast went black
and prisoners howled and children
ran through the night with candles,
who stood off motionless
side by side while the moon swam up
over the drowned houses?
Who neither touched nor spoke?
whose nape, whose finger-ends
nervelessly lied the hours away?

●

A voice presses at me.
If I give in it won't
be like the girl the bull rode,
all Rubens flesh and happy moans.
But to be wrestled like a boy
with tongue, hips, knees, nerves, brain . . .
with language?
He doesn't know. He's watching
breasts under a striped blouse,
his bull's head down. The old
wine pours again through my veins.

Goodnight. then. 'Night. Again
we turn our backs and weary
weary we let down.
Things take us hard, no question.
How do you make it, all the way
from here to morning? I touch
you, made of such nerve
and flare and pride and swallowed tears.
Go home. Come to bed. The skies
look in at us, stern.
And this is an old story.

I dreamed about the war.
We were all sitting at table
in a kitchen in Chicago.
The radio had just screamed
that Illinois was the target.
No one felt like leaving,
we sat by the open window
and talked in the sunset.
I'll tell you that joke tomorrow,
you said with your saddest smile,
if İ can remember.

The end is just a straw,
a feather furling slowly down,
floating to light by chance, a breath

on the long-loaded scales.
Posterity trembles like a leaf
and we go on making heirs and heirlooms.
The world, we have to make it,
my coexistent friend said, leaning
back in his cell.
Siberia vastly hulks
behind him, which he did not make.

Oh futile tenderness
of touch in a world like this!
how much longer, dear child,
do you think sex will matter?
There might have been a wedding
that never was:
two creatures sprung free
from castiron covenants.
Instead our hands and minds
erotically waver . . .
Lightness is unavailing.

Catalpas wave and spill
their dull strings across this murk of spring.
I ache, brilliantly.
Only where there is language is there world.
In the harp of my hair, compose me
a song. Death's in the air,
we all know that. Still, for an hour,
I'd like to be gay. How could a gay song go?
Why that's your secret, and it shall be mine.
We are our words, and black and bruised and blue.
Under our skins, we're laughing.

In triste veritas?
Take hold, sweet hands, come on . . .
Broken!
When you falter, all eludes.
This is a seasick way,
this almost/never touching, this

drawing-off, this to-and-fro.
Subtlety stalks in your eyes,
your tongue knows what it knows.
I want your secrets—I *will* have them out.
Seasick, I drop into the sea.

1966

Jerusalem

In my dream, children
are stoning other children
with blackened carob-pods
I dream my son is riding
on an old grey mare
to a half-dead war
on a dead-grey road
through the cactus and thistles
and dried brook-beds.

In my dream, children
are swaddled in smoke
and their uncut hair smolders
even here, here
where trees have no shade
and rocks have no shadow
trees have no memories
only the stones and
the hairs of the head.

I dream his hair is growing
and has never been shorn
from slender temples hanging
like curls of barbed wire
and his first beard is growing
smoldering like fire

his beard is smoke and fire
and I dream him riding
patiently to the war.

What I dream of the city
is how hard it is to leave
and how useless to walk
outside the blasted walls
picking up the shells
from a half-dead war
and I wake up in tears
and hear the sirens screaming
and the carob-tree is bare.

Balfour Street
July 1966

Charleston in the Eighteen-Sixties

Derived from the diaries of Mary Boykin Chesnut

He seized me by the waist and kissed my throat . . .
Your eyes, dear, are they grey or blue,
eyes of an angel?
The carts have passed already with their heaped
night-soil, we breathe again . . .
Is this what war is? Nitrate . . .
But smell the pear,
the jasmine, the violets.
Why does this landscape always sadden you?
Now the freshet is up on every side,
the river comes to our doors,
limbs of primeval trees dip in the swamp.

●

So we fool on into the black
cloud ahead of us.
Everything human glitters fever-bright—
the thrill of waking up
out of a stagnant life?
There seems a spell upon
your lovers,—all dead of wounds
or blown to pieces . . . Nitrate!
I'm writing, blind with tears of rage.
In vain. Years, death, depopulation, fears,
bondage—these shall all be borne.
No imagination to forestall woe.

1966

Night Watch

And now, outside, the walls
of black flint, eyeless.
How pale in sleep you lie.
Love: my love is just a breath
blown on the pane and dissolved.
Everything, even you,
cries silently for help, the web
of the spider is ripped with rain,
the geese fly on into the black cloud.
What can I do for you?
what can I do for you?
Can the touch of a finger mend
what a finger's touch has broken?
Blue-eyed now, yellow-haired,
I stand in my old nightmare
beside the track, while you,
and over and over and always you
plod into the deathcars.
Sometimes you smile at me

and I—I smile back at you.
How sweet the odor of the station-master's roses!
How pure, how poster-like the colors of this dream.

1967

For a Russian Poet

1. *The winter dream*

Everywhere, snow is falling. Your bandaged foot
drags across huge cobblestones, bells
hammer in distant squares.
Everything we stood against has conquered
and now we're part
of it all. *Life's the main thing,* I hear you say,
but a fog is spreading between this landmass
and the one your voice
mapped so long for me. All that's visible
is walls, endlessly yellow-grey, where
so many risks were taken, the shredded skies
slowly littering both our continents with
the only justice left, burying
footprints, bells and voices with all deliberate speed.

1967

2. *Summer in the country*

Now, again, every year for years: the life-and-death talk,
late August, forebodings
under the birches, along the water's edge
and between the typed lines

and evenings, tracing a pattern of absurd hopes
in broken nutshells
                              but this year we both

sit after dark with the radio
unable to read, unable to write

trying the blurred edges of broadcasts
for a little truth, taking a walk before bed
wondering what a man can do, asking that
at the verge of tears in a lightning-flash of loneliness.

3. *The demonstration*

"Natalya Gorbanevskaya
13/3 Novopeschanaya Street
Apartment 34

At noon we sit down quietly on the parapet
and unfurl our banners
                            almost immediately
the sound of police whistles
from all corners of Red Square
                                        we sit
quietly and offer no resistance—"

Is this your little boy—?

we will relive this over and over

the banners torn
from our hands
                    blood flowing
a great jagged torn place
in the silence of complicity

that much at least
we did here

In your flat, drinking tea
waiting for the police
your children asleep while you write
quickly, the letters you want to get off
before tomorrow

•

I'm a ghost at your table
touching poems in a script I can't read

we'll meet each other later

August 1968

Poem of Women

—from the Yiddish of Kadia Molodovsky

I

The faces of women long dead, of our family,
come back in the night, come in dreams to me saying:
We have kept our blood pure through long generations,
we brought it to you like a sacred wine
from the kosher cellars of our hearts.
And one of them whispers:
I remained deserted, when my two rosy apples
still hung on the tree
and I gritted away the long nights of waking between my white
    teeth.

I will go meet the grandmothers, saying:
Your sighs were the whips that lashed me
and drove my young life to the threshold
to escape from your kosher beds.
But wherever the street grows dark you pursue me—
wherever a shadow falls.

Your whimperings race like the autumn wind past me,
and your words are the silken cord
still binding my thoughts,
My life is a page ripped out of a holy book
and part of the first line is missing.

●

II

There are such spring-like nights here,
when a blade of grass pushes up through the soil
and the fresh dawn is a green pillow
under the skeleton of a dead horse.
And all the limbs of a woman plead for the ache of birth.
And women come down to lie like sick sheep
by the wells—to heal their bodies,
their faces blackened with year-long thirst for a child's cry

There are such spring-like nights here
when lightning pierces the black soil with silver knives
and pregnant women approach the white tables of the hospital
with quiet steps
and smile at the unborn child
and perhaps at death.

There are such spring-like nights here
when a blade of grass pushes up through the soil.

5:30 A.M.

Birds and periodic blood.
Old recapitulations.
The fox, panting, fire-eyed,
gone to earth in my chest.
How beautiful we are,
she and I, with our auburn
pelts, our trails of blood,
our miracle escapes,
our whiplash panic flogging us on
to new miracles!
They've supplied us with pills
for bleeding, pills for panic.

Wash them down the sink.
This is truth, then:
dull needle groping in the spinal fluid,
weak acid in the bottom of the cup,
foreboding, foreboding.
No one tells the truth about truth,
that it's what the fox
sees from her scuffled burrow:
dull-jawed, onrushing
killer, being that
inanely single-minded
will have our skins at last.

1967

Picnic

Sunday in Inwood Park
                    the picnic eaten
the chicken bones scattered
                    for the fox we'll never see
the children playing in the caves
My death is folded in my pocket
                    like a nylon raincoat
What kind of sunlight is it
                    that leaves the rocks so cold?

1967

The Book

—for Richard Howard

You, hiding there in your words
like a disgrace
the cast-off son of a family
whose face is written in theirs
who must not be mentioned
who calls collect three times a year
from obscure towns out-of-state
and whose calls are never accepted
You who had to leave alone
and forgot your shadow hanging under the stairs
let me tell you: I have been in the house
I have spoken to all of them
they will not pronounce your name
they only allude to you
rising and sitting, going or coming,
falling asleep and waking,
giving away in marriage or calling for water
on their deathbeds
their faces look into each other and see
you
when they write at night in their diaries they are writing
to you

1968

Abnegation

The red fox, the vixen
dancing in the half-light among the junipers,

wise-looking in a sexy way,
Egyptian-supple in her sharpness—
what does she want
with the dreams of dead vixens,
the apotheosis of Reynard,
the literature of fox-hunting?
Only in her nerves the past
sings, a thrill of self-preservation.
I go along down the road
to a house nailed together by Scottish
Covenanters, instinct mortified
in a virgin forest,
and she springs toward her den
every hair on her pelt alive
with tidings of the immaculate present.
They left me a westernness,
a birthright, a redstained, ravelled
afghan of sky.
She has no archives,
no heirlooms, no future
except death
and I could be more
her sister than theirs
who chopped their way across these hills
—a chosen people.

1968

Women

—for C.R.G.

My three sisters are sitting
on rocks of black obsidian.
For the first time, in this light, I can see who they are.

•

My first sister is sewing her costume for the procession.
She is going as the Transparent Lady
and all her nerves will be visible.

My second sister is also sewing,
at the seam over her heart which has never healed entirely.
At last, she hopes, this tightness in her chest will ease.

My third sister is gazing
at a dark-red crust spreading westward far out on the sea.
Her stockings are torn but she is beautiful.

1968

Implosions

The world's
not wanton
only wild and wavering

I wanted to choose words that even you
would have to be changed by

Take the word
of my pulse, loving and ordinary
Send out your signals, hoist
your dark scribbled flags
but take
my hand

All wars are useless to the dead

My hands are knotted in the rope
and I cannot sound the bell

My hands are frozen to the switch
and I cannot throw it

•

The foot is in the wheel

When it's finished and we're lying
in a stubble of blistered flowers
eyes gaping, mouths staring
dusted with crushed arterial blues

I'll have done nothing
even for you?

1968

On Edges

When the ice starts to shiver
all across the reflecting basin
or water-lily leaves
dissect a simple surface
the word *drowning* flows through me.
You built a glassy floor
that held me
as I leaned to fish for old
hooks and toothed tin cans,
stems lashing out like ties of
silk dressing-gowns
archangels of lake-light
gripped in mud.

Now you hand me a torn letter.
On my knees, in the ashes, I could never
fit these ripped-up flakes together.
In the taxi I am still piecing
what syllables I can
translating at top speed like a thinking machine
that types out *useless* as *monster*
and *history* as *lampshade*.

Crossing the bridge I need all my nerve
to trust to the man-made cables.

The blades on that machine
could cut you to ribbons
but its function is humane.
Is this all I can say of these
delicate hooks, scythe-curved intentions
you and I handle? I'd rather
taste blood, yours or mine, flowing
from a sudden slash, than cut all day
with blunt scissors on dotted lines
like the teacher told.

1968

The Observer

Completely protected on all sides
by volcanoes
a woman, darkhaired, in stained jeans
sleeps in central Africa.
In her dreams, her notebooks, still
private as maiden diaries,
the mountain gorillas move through their life term;
their gentleness survives
observation. Six bands of them
inhabit, with her, the wooded highland.
When I lay me down to sleep
unsheltered by any natural guardians
from the panicky life-cycle of my tribe
I wake in the old cellblock
observing the daily executions,
rehearsing the laws
I cannot subscribe to,
envying the pale gorilla-scented dawn

she wakes into, the stream where she washes her hair,
the camera-flash of her quiet
eye.

1968

Nightbreak

Something broken   Something
I need   By someone
I love   Next year
will I remember what
This anger   unreal
                         yet
has to be gone through
The sun to set
on this anger
                    I go on
head down   into it
The mountain pulsing
Into the oildrum   drops
the ball of fire.

Time is quiet   doesn't break things
or even wound   Things are in danger
from people   The frail clay lamps
of Mesopotamia
row on row under glass
in the ethnological section
little hollows for dried-
up oil   The refugees
with their identical
tales of escape   I don't
collect what I can't use   I need
what can be broken.

•

In the bed the pieces fly together
and the rifts fill   or else
my body is a list   of wounds
symmetrically placed
a village
blown open   by planes
that did not   finish the job
The enemy has   withdrawn
between raids   become invisible
there are
          no agencies
                    of relief
the darkness becomes utter
Sleep   cracked and flaking
sifts over the shaken   target

What breaks   is night
not day   The white
scar   splitting
over the east
The crack weeping
Time for the pieces
                    to move
dumbly back
          toward each other.

1968

Leaflets

1.

The big star, and that other
lonely on black glass
overgrown with frozen
lesions, endless night

the Coal Sack gaping
black veins of ice on the pane
spelling a word:
                    Insomnia
not manic but ordinary
to start out of sleep
turning off and on
this seasick neon
vision, this
division

the head clears of sweet smoke
and poison gas

life without caution
the only worth living
love for a man
love for a woman
love for the facts
protectless

that self-defense be not
the arm's first motion

memory not only
cards of identity

that I can live half a year
as I have never lived up to this time—
Chekhov coughing up blood almost daily
the steamer edging in toward the penal colony
chained men dozing on deck
five forest fires lighting the island

lifelong that glare, waiting.

●

2.

Your face
      stretched like a mask
                  begins to tear
as you speak of Che Guevara
Bolivia, Nanterre
I'm too young to be your mother
you're too young to be my brother

your tears are not political
they are real water, burning
as the tears of Telemachus
burned

Over Spanish Harlem the moon
swells up, a fire balloon
fire gnawing the edge
of this crushed-up newspaper

                      now
the bodies come whirling
coal-black, ash-white
out of torn windows
and the death columns blacken
                  whispering
Who'd choose this life?

We're fighting for a slash of recognition,
a piercing to the pierced heart.
Tell me what you are going through—

but the attention flickers and will flicker
a matchflame in poison air
a thread, a hair of light: sum of all answer
to the *Know that I exist!* of all existing things.

•

3.

If, says the Dahomeyan devil,
someone has courage to enter the fire
the young man will be restored to life.

If, the girl whispers,
I do not go into the fire
I will not be able to live with my soul.

(Her face calm and dark as amber
under the dyed butterfly turban
her back scarified in ostrich-skin patterns.)

4.

Crusaders' wind glinting
off linked scales of sea
ripping the ghostflags
galloping at the fortress
Acre, bloodcaked, lionhearted
raw vomit curdling in the sun
gray walkers walking
straying with a curbed intentness
in and out the inclosures
the gallows, the photographs
of dead Jewish terrorists, aged 15
their fading faces wide-eyed
and out in the crusading sunlight
gray strayers still straying
dusty paths
the mad who live in the dried-up moat
of the War Museum

what are we coming to
what wants these things of us
who wants them

•

5.

The strain of being born
    over and over has torn your smile into pieces
Often I have seen it broken
    and then re-membered
and wondered how a beauty
    so anarch, so ungelded
will be cared for in this world.
    I want to hand you this
leaflet streaming with rain or tears
    but the words coming clear
something you might find crushed into your hand
    after passing a barricade
and stuff in your raincoat pocket.
    I want this to reach you
who told me once that poetry is nothing sacred
    —no more sacred that is
than other things in your life—
    to answer yes, if life is uncorrupted
no better poetry is wanted.
    I want this to be yours
in the sense that if you find and read it
    it will be there in you already
and the leaflet then merely something
    to leave behind, a little leaf
in the drawer of a sublet room.
    What else does it come down to
but handing on scraps of paper
    little figurines or phials
no stronger than the dry clay they are baked in
    yet more than dry clay or paper
because the imagination crouches in them.
    If we needed fire to remind us
that all true images
    were scooped out of the mud
where our bodies curse and flounder
    then perhaps that fire is coming
to sponge away the scribes and time-servers
    and much that you wou'd have loved will be lost as well

before you could handle it and know it
    just as we almost miss each other
in the ill cloud of mistrust, who might have touched
    hands quickly, shared food or given blood
for each other. I am thinking how we can use what we have
    to invent what we need.

Winter–Spring 1968

Ghazals: Homage to Ghalib

7/12/68

—for Sheila Rotner

The clouds are electric in this university.
The lovers astride the tractor burn fissures through the hay.

When I look at that wall I shall think of you
and of what you did not paint there.

Only the truth makes the pain of lifting a hand worthwhile:
the prism staggering under the blows of the raga.

The vanishing-point is the point where he appears.
Two parallel tracks converge, yet there has been no wreck.

To mutilate privacy with a single foolish syllable
is to throw away the search for the one necessary word.

When you read these lines, think of me
and of what I have not written here.

7/13/68

The ones who camped on the slopes, below the bare summit,
saw differently from us, who breathed thin air and kept walking.

Sleeping back-to-back, man and woman, we were more conscious
than either of us awake and alone in the world.

These words are vapor-trails of a plane that has vanished;
by the time I write them out, they are whispering something else.

Do we still have to feel jealous of our creations?
Once they might have outlived us; in this world, we'll die together.

Don't look for me in the room I've left;
the photograph shows just a white rocking-chair, still rocking.

7/14/68: i

In Central Park we talked of our own cowardice.
How many times a day, in this city, are those words spoken?

The tears of the universe aren't all stars, Danton;
some are satellites of brushed aluminum and stainless steel.

He, who was temporary, has joined eternity;
he has deserted us, gone over to the other side.

In the Theatre of the Dust no actor becomes famous.
In the last scene they all are blown away like dust.

"It may be if I had known them I would have loved them."
You were American, Whitman, and those words are yours.

7/14/68: ii

Did you think I was talking about my life?
I was trying to drive a tradition up against the wall.

The field they burned over is greener than all the rest.
You have to watch it, he said, the sparks can travel the roots.

Shot back into this earth's atmosphere
our children's children may photograph these stones.

●

In the red wash of the darkroom, I see myself clearly;
when the print is developed and handed about, the face
                                        is nothing to me.

For us the work undoes itself over and over:
the grass grows back, the dust collects, the scar breaks open.

7/16/68: i

Blacked-out on a wagon, part of my life cut out forever—
five green hours and forty violet minutes.

A cold spring slowed our lilacs, till a surf broke
violet/white, tender and sensual, misread it if you dare.

I tell you, truth is, at the moment, here
burning outward through our skins.

Eternity streams through my body:
touch it with your hand and see.

Till the walls of the tunnel cave in
and the black river walks on our faces.

7/16/68: ii

When they mow the fields, I see the world reformed
as if by snow, or fire, or physical desire.

First snow. Death of the city. Ghosts in the air.
Your shade among the shadows, interviewing the mist.

The mail came every day, but letters were missing;
by this I knew things were not what they ought to be.

The trees in the long park blurring back
into Olmsted's original dream-work.

The impartial scholar writes me from under house arrest.
I hope you are rotting in hell, Montaigne you bastard.

7/17/68

Armitage of scrap-iron for the radiations of a moon.
Flower cast in metal, Picasso-woman, sister.

Two hesitant Luna moths regard each other
with the spots on their wings: fascinated.

To resign *yourself*—what an act of betrayal!
—to throw a runaway spirit back to the dogs.

When the ebb-tide pulls hard enough, we are all starfish.
The moon has her way with us, my companion in crime.

At the Aquarium that day, between the white whale's loneliness
and the groupers' mass promiscuities, only ourselves.

7/26/68: i

Last night you wrote on the wall: Revolution is poetry.
Today you needn't write; the wall has tumbled down.

We were taught to respect the appearance behind the reality.
Our senses were out on parole, under surveillance.

A pair of eyes imprisoned for years inside my skull
is burning its way outward, the headaches are terrible.

I'm walking through a rubble of broken sculpture, stumbling
here on the spine of a friend, there on the hand of a brother.

All those joinings! and yet we fought so hard to be unique.
Neither alone, nor in anyone's arms, will we end up sleeping.

7/26/: ii

A dead mosquito, flattened against a door;
his image could survive our comings and our goings.

LeRoi! Eldridge! listen to us, we are ghosts
condemned to haunt the cities where you want to be at home.

The white children turn black on the negative.
The summer clouds blacken inside the camera-skull.

Every mistake that can be made, we are prepared to make;
anything less would fall short of the reality we're dreaming.

Someone has always been desperate, now it's our turn—
we who were free to weep for Othello and laugh at Caliban.

I have learned to smell a *conservateur* a mile away:
they carry illustrated catalogues of all that there is to lose.

8/1/68

The order of the small town on the riverbank,
forever at war with the order of the dark and starlit soul.

Were you free then all along, Jim, free at last,
of everything but the white boy's fantasies?

We pleaded guilty till we saw what rectitude was like:
its washed hands, and dead nerve, and sclerotic eye.

I long ago stopped dreaming of pure justice, your honor—
my crime was to believe we could make cruelty obsolete.

The body has been exhumed from the burnt-out bunker;
the teeth counted, the contents of the stomach told over.

And you, Custer, the Squaw-killer, hero of primitive schoolrooms—
where are you buried, what is the condition of your bones?

8/4/68
                                        —*for Aijaz Ahmad*

If these are letters, they will have to be misread.
If scribblings on a wall, they must tangle with all the others.

Fuck reds   Black Power   Angel loves Rosita
—and a transistor radio answers in Spanish: *Night must fall.*

•

Prisoners, soldiers, crouching as always, writing,
explaining the unforgivable to a wife, a mother, a lover.

Those faces are blurred and some have turned away
to which I used to address myself so hotly.

How is it, Ghalib, that your grief, resurrected in pieces,
has found its way to this room from your dark house in Delhi?

When they read this poem of mine, they are translators.
Every existence speaks a language of its own.

8/8/68: i

From here on, all of us will be living
like Galileo turning his first tube at the stars.

Obey the little laws and break the great ones
is the preamble to their constitution.

Even to hope is to leap into the unknown,
under the mocking eyes of the way things are.

There's a war on earth, and in the skull, and in the glassy spaces,
between the existing and the non-existing.

I need to live each day through, have them and know them all,
though I can see from here where I'll be standing at the end.

8/8/68: ii

—for A.H.C.

A piece of thread ripped-out from a fierce design,
some weaving figured as magic against oppression.

I'm speaking to you as a woman to a man:
when your blood flows I want to hold you in my arms.

How did we get caught up fighting this forest fire,
we, who were only looking for a still place in the woods?

How frail we are, and yet, dispersed, always returning,
the barnacles they keep scraping from the warship's hull.

The hairs on your breast curl so lightly as you lie there,
while the strong heart goes on pounding in its sleep.

From

The Will to Change

1971

November 1968

Stripped
you're beginning to float free
up through the smoke of brushfires
and incinerators
the unleafed branches won't hold you
nor the radar aerials

You're what the autumn knew would happen
after the last collapse
of primary color
once the last absolutes were torn to pieces
you could begin

How you broke open, what sheathed you
until this moment
I know nothing about it
my ignorance of you amazes me
now that I watch you
starting to give yourself away
to the wind

1968

Study of History

Out there.   The mind of the river
as it might be you.

Lights   blotted by unseen hulls
repetitive shapes passing
dull foam crusting the margin

113

barges sunk below the water-line with silence.
The scow, drudging on.

Lying in the dark, to think of you
and your harsh traffic
gulls pecking your rubbish   natural historians
mourning your lost purity
pleasure cruisers
witlessly careening you

but this
after all
is the narrows and after
all we have never entirely
known what was done to you upstream
what powers trepanned
which of your channels diverted
what rockface leaned to stare
in your upturned
defenseless
face.

1968

Planetarium

Thinking of Caroline Herschel (1750–1848)
astronomer, sister of William; and others.

A woman in the shape of a monster
a monster in the shape of a woman
the skies are full of them

a woman   'in the snow
among the Clocks and instruments
or measuring the ground with poles'

●

in her 98 years to discover
8 comets

she whom the moon ruled
like us
levitating into the night sky
riding the polished lenses

Galaxies of women, there
doing penance for impetuousness
ribs chilled
in those spaces   of the mind

An eye,

        'virile, precise and absolutely certain'
        from the mad webs of Uranusborg

                                        encountering the NOVA

every impulse of light exploding
from the core
as life flies out of us

        Tycho whispering at last
        'Let me not seem to have lived in vain'

What we see, we see
and seeing is changing

the light that shrivels a mountain
and leaves a man alive

Heartbeat of the pulsar
heart sweating through my body

The radio impulse
pouring in from Taurus

    •

I am bombarded yet   I stand

I have been standing all my life in the
direct path of a battery of signals
the most accurately transmitted most
untranslatable language in the universe
I am a galactic cloud so deep   so invo-
luted that a light wave could take 15
years to travel through me   And has
taken   I am an instrument in the shape
of a woman trying to translate pulsations
into images   for the relief of the body
and the reconstruction of the mind.

1968

The Burning of Paper Instead of Children

> *I was in danger of*
> *verbalizing my moral*
> *impulses out of existence.*
> *—Daniel Berrigan,*
> *on trial in Baltimore.*

1. My neighbor, a scientist and art-collector, telephones me in a
state of violent emotion. He tells me that my son and his, aged
eleven and twelve, have on the last day of school burned a mathe-
matics textbook in the backyard. He has forbidden my son to come
to his house for a week, and has forbidden his own son to leave the
house during that time. "The burning of a book," he says, "arouses
terrible sensations in me, memories of Hitler; there are few things
that upset me so much as the idea of burning a book."

Back there: the library, walled
with green Britannicas
Looking again

in Dürer's *Complete Works*
for MELANCOLIA, the baffled woman

the crocodiles in Herodotus
the Book of the Dead
the *Trial of Jeanne d'Arc,* so blue
I think, It is her color

and they take the book away
because I dream of her too often

love and fear in a house
knowledge of the oppressor
I know it hurts to burn

2. To imagine a time of silence
or few words
a time of chemistry and music

the hollows above your buttocks
traced by my hand
or, *hair is like flesh,* you said

an age of long silence

relief

from this tongue   this slab of limestone
or reinforced concrete
fanatics and traders
dumped on this coast wildgreen clayred
that breathed once
in signals of smoke
sweep of the wind

knowledge of the oppressor
this is the oppressor's language

yet I need it to talk to you

●

3. *People suffer highly in poverty and it takes dignity and intelli-
gence to overcome this suffering. Some of the suffering are: a child
did not had dinner last night: a child steal because he did not have
money to buy it: to hear a mother say she do not have money to buy
food for her children and to see a child without cloth it will make
tears in your eyes.*

(the fracture of order
the repair of speech
to overcome this suffering)

4. We lie under the sheet
after making love, speaking
of loneliness
relieved in a book
relived in a book
so on that page
the clot and fissure
of it appears
words of a man
in pain
a naked word
entering the clot
a hand grasping
through bars:

deliverance

What happens between us
has happened for centuries
we know it from literature

still it happens

sexual jealousy
outflung hand
beating bed

dryness of mouth
after panting

●

there are books that describe all this
and they are useless

You walk into the woods behind a house
there in that country
you find a temple
built eighteen hundred years ago
you enter without knowing
what it is you enter

so it is with us

no one knows what may happen
though the books tell everything

burn the texts   said Artaud

5. I am composing on the typewriter late at night, thinking of
today. How well we all spoke. A language is a map of our failures.
Frederick Douglass wrote an English purer than Milton's. People
suffer highly in poverty. There are methods but we do not use them.
Joan, who could not read, spoke some peasant form of French.
Some of the suffering are: it is hard to tell the truth; this is America;
I cannot touch you now. In America we have only the present tense.
I am in danger. You are in danger. The burning of a book arouses
no sensation in me. I know it hurts to burn. There are flames of
napalm in Catonsville, Maryland. I know it hurts to burn. The
typewriter is overheated, my mouth is burning, I cannot touch you
and this is the oppressor's language.

1968

I Dream I'm the Death of Orpheus

I am walking rapidly through striations of light and dark thrown
     under an arcade.

I am a woman in the prime of life, with certain powers
and those powers severely limited

by authorities whose faces I rarely see.
I am a woman in the prime of life
driving her dead poet in a black Rolls-Royce
through a landscape of twilight and thorns.
A woman with a certain mission
which if obeyed to the letter will leave her intact.
A woman with the nerves of a panther
a woman with contacts among Hell's Angels
a woman feeling the fullness of her powers
at the precise moment when she must not use them
a woman sworn to lucidity
who sees through the mayhem, the smoky fires
of these underground streets
her dead poet learning to walk backward against the wind
on the wrong side of the mirror

1968

The Blue Ghazals

9/21/68

Violently asleep in the old house.
A clock stays awake all night ticking.

Turning, turning their bruised leaves
the trees stay awake all night in the wood.

Talk to me with your body through my dreams.
Tell me what we are going through.

The walls of the room are muttering,
old trees, old Utopians, arguing with the wind.

To float like a dead man in a sea of dreams
and half those dreams being dreamed by someone else.

●

Fifteen years of sleepwalking with you,
wading against the tide, and with the tide.

9/23/68

One day of equinoctial light after another,
moving ourselves through gauzes and fissures of that light.

Early and late I come and set myself against you,
your phallic fist knocking blindly at my door.

The dew is beaded like mercury on the coarsened grass,
the web of the spider is heavy as if with sweat.

Everything is yielding toward a foregone conclusion,
only we are rash enough to go on changing our lives.

An Ashanti woman tilts the flattened basin on her head
to let the water slide downward: I am that woman
        and that water.

9/28/68

A man, a woman, a city.
The city as object of love.

Anger and filth in the basement.
The furnace stoked and blazing.

A sexual heat on the pavements.
Trees erected like statues.

Eyes at the ends of avenues.
Yellow for hesitation.

I'm tired of walking your streets
he says, unable to leave her.

Air of dust and rising sparks,
the city burning her letters.

12/13/68

They say, if you can tell, clasped tight under the blanket,
the edge of dark from the edge of dawn, your love is a lie.

If I thought of my words as changing minds,
hadn't my mind also to suffer changes?

They measure fever, swab the blisters of the throat,
but the cells of thought go rioting on ignored.

It's the inner ghost that suffers, little spirit
looking out wildly from the clouded pupils.

When will we lie clearheaded in our flesh again
with the cold edge of the night driving us close together?

12/20/68: i

There are days when I seem to have nothing
but these frayed packets, done up with rotting thread.

The shortest day of the year, let it be ours.
Let me give you something: a token for the subway.

(Refuse even
the most beloved old solutions.

That dead man wrote, grief ought to reach the lips.
You must believe I know before you can tell me.

A black run through the tunnelled winter, he and she,
together, touching, yet not side by side.

5/4/69

Pain made her conservative.
Where the matches touched her flesh, she wears a scar.

The police arrive at dawn
like death and childbirth.

•

City of accidents, your true map
is the tangling of all our lifelines.

The moment when a feeling enters the body
is political. This touch is political.

Sometimes I dream we are floating on water
hand-in-hand; and sinking without terror.

Pierrot Le Fou

1.

Suppose you stood facing
a wall
　　　　of photographs
from your unlived life

as you stand looking at these
stills from the unseen film?

Yourself against a wall
curiously stuccoed

Yourself in the doorway
of a kind of watchman's hut

Yourself at a window
signalling to people
you haven't met yet

Yourself in unfamiliar clothes
with the same eyes

2.

On a screen as wide as this, I grope for the titles.
I speak the French language like a schoolgirl of the 'forties.

Those roads remind me of Beauce and the motorcycle.
We rode from Paris to Chartres in the March wind.
He said we should go to Spain but the wind defeated me.
France of the superhighways, I never knew you.
How much the body took in those days, and could take!
A naked lightbulb still simmers in my eyeballs.
In every hotel, I lived on the top floor.

3.

Suppose we had time
and no money
living by our wits
              telling stories

which stories would you tell?

I would tell the story
of Pierrot Le Fou
who trusted
          not a woman
                  but love itself

till his head blew off
not quite intentionally

I would tell all the stories I knew
in which people went wrong
but the nervous system

was right all along

4.

The island blistered our feet.
At first we mispronounced each others' names.
All the leaves of the tree were scribbled with words.
There was a language there but no-one to speak it.
Sometimes each of us was alone.
At noon on the beach our shadows left us.

The net we twisted from memory kept on breaking.
The damaged canoe lay on the beach like a dead animal.
You started keeping a journal on a coconut shell.

5.

When I close my eyes
other films
                    have been there all along—

a market shot:
bins of turnips, feet
of dead chickens
close-up: a black old woman
buying voodoo medicines

a figure of terrible faith
and I know her needs

Another film:
                    an empty room stacked with old films
I am kneeling on the floor
it is getting dark
                    they want to close the building
and I still haven't found you

Scanning reel after reel
tundras in negative,
the Bowery
            all those scenes

but the light is failing
                    and you are missing
from the footage of the march
the railway disaster
the snowbound village

even the shots of the island
miss you
            yet you were there

●

6.

To record
in order to see

if you know how the story ends
why tell it

To record
in order to forget

the surface is always lucid
my shadows are under the skin

To record
in order to control

the eye of the camera
doesn't weep tears of blood

To record
for that is what one does

climbing your stairs, over and over
I memorized the bare walls

This is my way of coming back

1969

Letters: March 1969

1.

Foreknown. The victor
sees the disaster through and through.
His soles grind rocksalt
from roads of the resistance.
He shoulders through rows
of armored faces
he might have loved and lived among.
The victory carried like a corpse
from town to town

begins to crawl in the casket.
The summer swindled on
from town to town, our train
stopping and broiling on the rails
long enough to let on who we were.
The disaster sat up with us all night
drinking bottled water, eating fruit,
talking of the conditions that prevailed.
Outside along the railroad cut
they were singing for our death.

2.

Hopes sparkle like water in the clean carafe.
How little it takes
to restore composure.
White napkins, a tray
of napoleons and cherry tarts
compliments of the airline
which has flown us out of danger.
They are torturing the journalist we drank with
last night in the lounge
but we can't be sure of that
here overlooking the runway
three hours and twenty minutes into another life.
If this is done for us
(and this is done for us)
if we are well men wearing bandages
for disguise
if we can choose our scene
stay out of earshot
break the roll and pour
from the clean carafe
if we can desert like soldiers
abjure like thieves
we may well purchase new virtues at the gate
of the other world.

•

3.

"I am up at sunrise
collecting data.
The reservoir burns green.
Darling, the knives they have on this block alone
would amaze you.
When they ask my profession I say
I'm a student of weapons systems.
The notes I'm putting together are purely
of sentimental value
my briefcase is I swear useless
to foreign powers, to the police
I am not given I say
to revealing my sources
to handing round copies
of my dossier for perusal.
The vulnerable go unarmed.
I myself walk the floor
a ruinously expensive Swiss hunting knife
exposed in my brain
eight blades, each one for a distinct purpose,
laid open as on the desk
of an importer or a fence."

4.

Six months back
send carbons you said
but this winter's dashed off in pencil
torn off the pad too fast
for those skills. In the dawn taxi
in the kitchen
burning the succotash
the more I love my life the more
I love you. In a time
of fear. In a city
of fears. In a life
without vacations the paisley fades

winter and summer in the sun
but the best time is now.

My sick friend writes: *what's love?*
This life is nothing, Adrienne!

Her hands bled onto the sill.
She had that trick of reaching outward,
the pane was smashed but only
the calvinist northwind
spat in from the sea.
She's a shot hero. A dying poet.
Even now, if we went for her—
but they've gone with rags and putty to fix the pane.
She stays in with her mirrors and anger.

I tear up answers
I once gave, postcards
from riot and famine go up on the walls
valentines stuck in the mirror
flame and curl, loyalties dwindle
the bleak light dries our tears
without relief. I keep coming back to you

in my head, but you couldn't know that, and
I have no carbons. Prince of pity,
what eats out of your hand?
the rodent pain, electric
with exhaustion, mazed and shaken?
I'd have sucked the wound in your hand to sleep
but my lips were trembling.
Tell me how to bear myself,
how it's done, the light kiss falling
accurately
on the cracked palm.

1969

Pieces

1. *Breakpoint*

The music of words
received as fact

The steps that wouldn't hold us both
splintering in air.

The self witheld in an urn
like ashes

To have loved you better than you loved yourself
—whoever you were, to have loved you—

And still to love but simply
as one of those faces on the street

2. *Relevance*

That erudition
how to confront it

The critics wrote answers
the questions were ours

A breast, a shoulder
chilled at waking

The cup of yogurt
eaten at noon
and no explanations

The books we borrowed
trying to read each other's minds

●

Paperbacks piling
on both sides of the fireplace
and piled beside the bed

What difference could it make
that those books came
out of unintelligible pain

as daylight out of the hours

when that light burned
atop the insurance tower
all night like the moon

3. *Memory*

Plugged-in to her body
he came the whole way
but it makes no difference

If not this then what
would fuse a connection

(All that burning intelligence about love
what can it matter

Falling in love on words
and ending in silence
with its double-meanings

Always falling and ending
because this world gives no room
to be what we dreamt of being

Are we, as he said
of the generation that forgets
the lightning-flash, the air-raid

and each other

•

4. *Time and Place*

Liquid mist burning off
along the highway

Slap of water
Light on shack boards

Hauling of garbage
early in the wet street

Always the same, wherever waking,
the old positions
assumed by the mind

and the new day forms
like a china cup

hard, cream-colored, unbreakable
even in our travels

5. *Revelation*

This morning: read Simone Weil
on the loss of grace

drank a glass of water

remembered the dream that woke me:

some one, some more than one
battering into my room
intent to kill me

I crying your name
its two syllables
ringing through sleep

knowing it vain
knowing
you slept unhearing

•

crying your name
like a spell

like signs executed

by the superstitious

who are the faithful of this world

1969

Our Whole Life

Our whole life a translation
the permissible fibs

and now a knot of lies
eating at itself to get undone

Words bitten thru words

meanings burnt-off like paint
under the blowtorch

All those dead letters
rendered into the oppressor's language

Trying to tell the doctor where it hurts
like the Algerian
who walked from his village, burning

his whole body a cloud of pain
and there are no words for this

except himself

1969

The Stelae

—for Arnold Rich

Last night I met you in my sister's house
risen from the dead
showing me your collection

You are almost at the point of giving things away

It's the stelae on the walls I want
that I never saw before

You offer other objects
I have seen time and time again

I think you think you are giving me
something precious

The stelae are so unlike you
swart, indifferent, incised with signs
you have never deciphered

I never knew you had them
I wonder if you are giving them away

1969

The Photograph of the Unmade Bed

Cruelty is rarely conscious
One slip of the tongue

●

one exposure
among so many

a thrust in the dark
to see if there's pain there

I never asked you to explain
that act of violence

what dazed me was our ignorance
of our will to hurt each other

      . . . . . .

          In a flash I understand
          how poems are unlike photographs

          (the one saying   *This could be*
          the other   *This was*

          The image
          isn't responsible

          for our uses of it
          It is intentionless

          A long strand of dark hair
          in the washbasin

          is innocent and yet
          such things have done harm

     . . . . . .

These snapshots taken by ghetto children
given for Christmas

Objects blurring into perceptions
No 'art,' only the faults

    ●

of the film, the faults of the time
Did mere indifference blister

these panes, eat these walls,
shrivel and scrub these trees—

mere indifference? I tell you
cruelty is rarely conscious

the done and the undone blur
into one photograph of failure

. . . . . .

This crust of bread we try to share
this name traced on a window

this word I paste together
like a child fumbling

with paste and scissors
this writing in the sky with smoke

this silence

this lettering chalked on the ruins
this alphabet of the dumb

this feather held to lips
that still breathe and are warm

1969

A Valediction Forbidding Mourning

My swirling wants. Your frozen lips.
The grammar turned and attacked me.

Themes, written under duress.
Emptiness of the notations.

They gave me a drug that slowed the healing of wounds.

I want you to see this before I leave:
the experience of repetition as death
the failure of criticism to locate the pain
the poster in the bus that said:
my bleeding is under control.

A red plant in a cemetery of plastic wreaths.

A last attempt: the language is a dialect called metaphor.
These images go unglossed: hair, glacier, flashlight.
When I think of a landscape I am thinking of a time.
When I talk of taking a trip I mean forever.
I could say: those mountains have a meaning
but further than that I could not say.

To do something very common, in my own way.

1970

Shooting Script

PART I 11/69–2/70

1.

We were bound on the wheel of an endless conversation.

Inside this shell, a tide waiting for someone to enter.

A monologue waiting for you to interrupt it.

A man wading into the surf. The dialogue of the rock with the breaker.

●

The wave changed instantly by the rock; the rock changed by the wave returning over and over.

The dialogue that lasts all night or a whole lifetime.

A conversation of sounds melting constantly into rhythms.

A shell waiting for you to listen.

A tide that ebbs and flows against a deserted continent.

A cycle whose rhythm begins to change the meanings of words.

A wheel of blinding waves of light, the spokes pulsing out from where we hang together in the turning of an endless conversation.

The meaning that searches for its word like a hermit crab.

A monologue that waits for one listener.

An ear filled with one sound only.

A shell penetrated by meaning.

2.

Adapted from Mirza Ghalib

Even when I thought I prayed, I was talking to myself; when I found the door shut, I simply walked away.

We all accept Your claim to be unique; the stone lips, the carved limbs, were never your true portrait.

Grief held back from the lips wears at the heart; the drop that refused to join the river dried up in the dust.

Now tell me your story till the blood drips from your lashes. Any other version belongs to your folklore, or ours.

●

To see the Tigris in a water-drop . . . Either you were playing games with me, or you never cared to learn the structure of my language.

3.

The old blanket. The crumbs of rubbed wool turning up.

Where we lay and breakfasted. The stains of tea. The squares of winter light projected on the wool.

You, sleeping with closed windows. I, sleeping in the silver nitrate burn of zero air.

Where it can snow, I'm at home; the crystals accumulating spell out my story.

The cold encrustation thickening on the ledge.

The arrow-headed facts, accumulating, till a whole city is taken over.

Midwinter and the loss of love, going comes before gone, over and over the point is missed and still the blind will turns for its target.

4.

In my imagination I was the pivot of a fresh beginning.

In rafts they came over the sea; on the island they put up those stones by methods we can only guess at.

If the vegetation grows as thick as this, how can we see what they were seeing?

It is all being made clear, with bulldozers, at Angkor Wat.

The verdure was a false mystery; the baring of the stones is no solution for us now.

●

Defoliation progresses; concrete is poured, sheets of glass hauled
overland in huge trucks and at great cost.

Here we never travailed, never took off our shoes to walk the
final mile.

Come and look into this cellar-hole; this is the foundling of the
woods.

Humans lived here once; it became sacred only when they went
away.

5.

Of simple choice they are the villagers; their clothes come with
them like red clay roads they have been walking.

The sole of the foot is a map, the palm of the hand a letter,
learned by heart and worn close to the body.

They seemed strange to me, till I began to recall their dialect.

Poking the spade into the dry loam, listening for the tick of
broken pottery, hoarding the brown and black bits in a dented can.

Evenings, at the table, turning the findings out, pushing them
around with a finger, beginning to dream of fitting them together.

Hiding all this work from them, although they might have helped
me.

Going up at night, hiding the tin can in a closet, where the linoleum
lies in shatters on a back shelf.

Sleeping to dream of the unformed, the veil of water pouring over
the wet clay, the rhythms of choice, the lost methods.

•

6.

You are beside me like a wall; I touch you with my fingers and
keep moving through the bad light.

At this time of year when faces turn aside, it is amazing that your
eyes are to be met.

A bad light is one like this, that flickers and diffuses itself along
the edge of a frontier.

No, I don't invest you with anything; I am counting on your
weakness as much as on your strength.

This light eats away at the clarities I had fixed on; it moves up
like a rodent at the edge of the raked paths.

Your clarities may not reach me; but your attention will.

It is to know that I too have no mythic powers; it is to see the
liability of all my treasures.

You will have to see all this for a long time alone.

You are beside me like a wall; I touch you with my fingers and
keep trying to move through the bad light.

PART II 3–7/70

9.

NEWSREEL

This would not be the war we fought in. See, the foliage is
heavier, there were no hills of that size there.

But I find it impossible not to look for actual persons known
to me and not seen since; impossible not to look for myself.

•

The scenery angers me, I know there is something wrong, the sun
is too high, the grass too trampled, the peasants' faces too broad,
and the main square of the capital had no arcades like those.

Yet the dead look right, and the roofs of the huts, and the crashed
fuselage burning among the ferns.

But this is not the war I came to see, buying my ticket, stumbling
through the darkness, finding my place among the sleepers and
masturbators in the dark.

I thought of seeing the General who cursed us, whose name they
gave to an expressway; I wanted to see the faces of the dead when
they were living.

Once I know they filmed us, back at the camp behind the lines,
taking showers under the trees and showing pictures of our girls.

Somewhere there is a film of the war we fought in, and it must
contain the flares, the souvenirs, the shadows of the netted brush,
the standing in line of the innocent, the hills that were not of
this size.

Somewhere my body goes taut under the deluge, somewhere I am
naked behind the lines, washing my body in the water of that war.

Someone has that war stored up in metal canisters, a memory he
cannot use, somewhere my innocence is proven with my guilt, but
this would not be the war I fought in.

10.
                                          —for Valerie Glauber

They come to you with their descriptions of your soul.

They come and drop their mementos at the foot of your bed; their
feathers, ferns, fans, grasses from the western mountains.

●

They wait for you to unfold for them like a paper flower, a secret
springing open in a glass of water.

They believe your future has a history and that it is themselves.

They have family trees to plant for you, photographs of dead
children, old bracelets and rings they want to fasten onto you.

And, in spite of this, you live alone.

Your secret hangs in the open like Poe's purloined letter; their
longing and their methods will never let them find it.

Your secret cries out in the dark and hushes; when they start out
of sleep they think you are innocent.

You hang among them like the icon in a Russian play; living your
own intenser life behind the lamp they light in front of you.

You are spilt here like mercury on a marble counter, liquefying
into many globes, each silvered like a planet caught in a lens.

You are a mirror lost in a brook, an eye reflecting a torrent of
reflections.

You are a letter written, folded, burnt to ash, and mailed in an
envelope to another continent.

11.

The mare's skeleton in the clearing: another sign of life.

When you pull the embedded bones up from the soil, the flies
collect again.

The pelvis, the open archway, staring at me like an eye.

In the desert these bones would be burnt white; a green bloom grows
on them in the woods.

Did she break her leg or die of poison?

What was it like when the scavengers came?

So many questions unanswered, yet the statement is here and clear.

With what joy you handled the skull, set back the teeth spilt in the
grass, hinged back the jaw on the jaw.

With what joy we left the woods, swinging our sticks, miming the
speech of noble savages, of the fathers of our country, bursting
into the full sun of the uncut field.

12.

I was looking for a way out of a lifetime's consolations.

We walked in the wholesale district: closed warehouses, windows,
steeped in sun.

I said: those cloths are very old. You said: they have lain in
that window a long time.

When the skeletons of the projects shut off the sunset, when the
sense of the Hudson leaves us, when only by loss of light in the east
do I know that I am living in the west.

When I give up being paraphrased, when I let go, when the
beautiful solutions in their crystal flasks have dried up in the sun,
when the lightbulb bursts on lighting, when the dead bulb rattles
like a seed-pod.

Those cloths are very old, they are mummies' cloths, they have lain
in graves, they were not intended to be sold, the tragedy of this
mistake will soon be clear.

Vacillant needles of Manhattan, describing hour & weather; buying
these descriptions at the cost of missing every other point.

•

13.

We are driven to odd attempts; once it would not have occurred to me to put out in a boat, not on a night like this.

Still, it was an instrument, and I had pledged myself to try any instrument that came my way. Never to refuse one from conviction of incompetence.

A long time I was simply learning to handle the skiff; I had no special training and my own training was against me.

I had always heard that darkness and water were a threat.

In spite of this, darkness and water helped me to arrive here.

I watched the lights on the shore I had left for a long time; each one, it seemed to me, was a light I might have lit, in the old days.

14.

Whatever it was: the grains of the glacier caked in the boot-cleats; ashes spilled on white formica.

The death-col viewed through power-glasses; the cube of ice melting on stainless steel.

Whatever it was, the image that stopped you, the one on which you came to grief, projecting it over & over on empty walls.

Now to give up the temptations of the projector; to see instead the web of cracks filtering across the plaster.

To read there the map of the future, the roads radiating from the initial split, the filaments thrown out from that impasse.

To reread the instructions on your palm; to find there how the lifeline, broken, keeps its direction.

●

To read the etched rays of the bullet-hole left years ago in the glass; to know in every distortion of the light what fracture is.

To put the prism in your pocket, the thin glass lens, the map of the inner city, the little book with gridded pages.

To pull yourself up by your own roots; to eat the last meal in your old neighborhood.

From

Diving into the Wreck

1973

Trying to Talk with a Man

Out in this desert we are testing bombs,

that's why we came here.

Sometimes I feel an underground river
forcing its way between deformed cliffs
an acute angle of understanding
moving itself like a locus of the sun
into this condemned scenery.

What we've had to give up to get here—
whole LP collections, films we starred in
playing in the neighborhoods, bakery windows
full of dry, chocolate-filled Jewish cookies,
the language of love-letters, of suicide notes,
afternoons on the riverbank
pretending to be children

Coming out to this desert
we meant to change the face of
driving among dull green succulents
walking at noon in the ghost town
surrounded by a silence

that sounds like the silence of the place
except that it came with us
and is familiar
and everything we were saying until now
was an effort to blot it out—
coming out here we are up against it

Out here I feel more helpless
with you than without you

You mention the danger
and list the equipment
we talk of people caring for each other
in emergencies—laceration, thirst—
but you look at me like an emergency

Your dry heat feels like power
your eyes are stars of a different magnitude
they reflect lights that spell out: EXIT
when you get up and pace the floor

talking of the danger
as if it were not ourselves
as if we were testing anything else.

1971

When We Dead Awaken

—for E.Y.

Trying to tell you how
the anatomy of the park
through stained panes, the way
guerrillas are advancing
through minefields, the trash
burning endlessly in the dump
to return to heaven like a stain—
everything outside our skins is an image
of this affliction:
stones on my table, carried by hand
from scenes I trusted
souvenirs of what I once described
as happiness
everything outside my skin
speaks of the fault that sends me limping
even the scars of my decisions

even the sunblaze in the mica-vein
even you, fellow-creature, sister,
sitting across from me, dark with love,
working like me to pick apart
working with me to remake
this trailing knitted thing, this cloth of darkness,
this woman's garment, trying to save the skein.

2.

The fact of being separate
enters your livelihood like a piece of furniture
—a chest of seventeenth-century wood
from somewhere in the North.
It has a huge lock shaped like a woman's head
but the key has not been found.
In the compartments are other keys
to lost doors, an eye of glass.
Slowly you begin to add
things of your own.
You come and go reflected in its panels.
You give up keeping track of anniversaries,
you begin to write in your diaries
more honestly than ever.

3.

The lovely landscape of southern Ohio
betrayed by strip mining, the
thick gold band on the adulterer's finger
the blurred programs of the offshore pirate station
are causes for hesitation.
Here in the matrix of need and anger, the
disproof of what we thought possible
failures of medication
doubts of another's existence
—tell it over and over, the words
get thick with unmeaning—
yet never have we been closer to the truth
of the lies we were living, listen to me:

the faithfulness I can imagine would be a weed
flowering in tar, a blue energy piercing
the massed atoms of a bedrock disbelief.

1971

Waking in the Dark

1.

The thing that arrests me is
   how we are composed of molecules

     (he showed me the figure in the paving stones)

   arranged without our knowledge and consent

      like the wirephoto composed
      of millions of dots

      in which the man from Bangladesh
      walks starving
         on the front page
         knowing nothing about it

      which is his presence for the world

2.

We were standing in line outside of something
two by two, or alone in pairs, or simply alone,
looking into windows full of scissors,
windows full of shoes. The street was closing,
the city was closing, would we be the lucky ones
to make it? They were showing
in a glass case, the Man Without A Country.
We held up our passports in his face, we wept for him.

    ●

They are dumping animal blood into the sea
to bring up the sharks. Sometimes every
aperture of my body
leaks blood. I don't know whether
to pretend that this is natural.
Is there a law about this, a law of nature?
You worship the blood
you call it hysterical bleeding
you want to drink it like milk
you dip your finger into it and write
you faint at the smell of it
you dream of dumping me into the sea.

3.

The tragedy of sex
lies around us, a woodlot
the axes are sharpened for.
The old shelters and huts
stare through the clearing with a certain resolution
—the hermit's cabin, the hunters' shack—
scenes of masturbation
and dirty jokes.
A man's world. But finished.
They themselves have sold it to the machines.
I walk the unconscious forest,
a woman dressed in old army fatigues
that have shrunk to fit her, I am lost
at moments, I feel dazed
by the sun pawing between the trees,
cold in the bog and lichen of the thicket.
Nothing will save this. I am alone,
kicking the last rotting logs
with their strange smell of life, not death,
wondering what on earth it all might have become.

●

4.

Clarity,
        spray
blinding and purging

spears of sun striking the water

the bodies riding the air

like gliders

the bodies in slow motion

falling
into the pool
at the Berlin Olympics

control; loss of control

the bodies rising
arching back to the tower
time reeling backward

clarity of open air
before the dark chambers
with the shower-heads

the bodies falling again
freely

               faster than light
the water opening
like air
like realization

A woman made this film
against

the law
of gravity

•

5.

All night dreaming of a body
space weighs on differently from mine
We are making love in the street
the traffic flows off from us
pouring back like a sheet
the asphalt stirs with tenderness
there is no dismay
we move together like underwater plants

Over and over, starting to wake
I dive back to discover you
still whispering, *touch me,* we go on
streaming through the slow
citylight forest ocean
stirring our body hair

But this is the saying of a dream
on waking
I wish there were somewhere
actual we could stand
handing the power-glasses back and forth
looking at the earth, the wildwood
where the split began

1971

Incipience

1. To live, to lie awake
under scarred plaster
while ice is forming over the earth
at an hour when nothing can be done
to further any decision

•

to know the composing of the thread
inside the spider's body
first atoms of the web
visible tomorrow

to feel the fiery future
of every matchstick in the kitchen

Nothing can be done
but by inches. I write out my life
hour by hour, word by word
gazing into the anger of old women on the bus
numbering the striations
of air inside the ice cube
imagining the existence
of something uncreated
this poem
our lives

2. A man is asleep in the next room
       We are his dreams
       We have the heads and breasts of women
       the bodies of birds of prey
       Sometimes we turn into silver serpents
While we sit up smoking and talking of how to live
he turns on the bed and murmurs

A man is asleep in the next room
       A neurosurgeon enters his dream
       and begins to dissect his brain
       She does not look like a nurse
       she is absorbed in her work
       she has a stern, delicate face like Marie Curie
She is not/might be either of us

A man is asleep in the next room
       He has spent a whole day
       standing, throwing stones into the black pool
       which keeps its blackness

Outside the frame of his dream we are stumbling up the hill
    hand in hand, stumbling and guiding each other
    over the scarred volcanic rock

1971

After Twenty Years

—for A. P. C.

Two women sit at a table by a window. Light breaks
unevenly on both of them.
Their talk is a striking of sparks
which passers-by in the street observe
as a glitter in the glass of that window.
Two women in the prime of life.
Their babies are old enough to have babies.
Loneliness has been part of their story for twenty years,
the dark edge of the clever tongue,
the obscure underside of the imagination.
It is snow and thunder in the street.
While they speak the lightning flashes purple.
It is strange to be so many women,
eating and drinking at the same table,
those who bathed their children in the same basin
who kept their secrets from each other
walked the floors of their lives in separate rooms
and flow into history now as the woman of their time
living in the prime of life
as in a city where nothing is forbidden
and nothing permanent.

1971

From the Prison House

Underneath my lids another eye has opened
it looks nakedly
at the light

that soaks in from the world of pain
even when I sleep

Steadily it regards
everything I am going through

and more

it sees the clubs and rifle-butts
rising and falling
it sees

detail not on TV

the fingers of the policewoman
searching the cunt of the young prostitute
it sees

the roaches dropping into the pan
where they cook the pork
in the House of D

it sees
the violence
embedded in silence

This eye
is not for weeping
its vision

must be unblurred
though tears are on my face

its intent is clarity
it must forget
nothing

1971

The Mirror in Which
Two Are Seen as One

1.

She is the one you call sister.
Her simplest act has glamor,
as when she scales a fish the knife
flashes in her long fingers
no motion wasted or when
rapidly talking of love
she steel-wool burnishes
the battered kettle

Love apples cramp you sideways
with sudden emptiness
the cereals glutting you, the grains
ripe clusters picked by hand
Love: the refrigerator
with open door
the ripe steaks bleeding
their hearts out in plastic film
the whipped butter, the apricots
the sour leftovers

A crate is waiting in the orchard
for you to fill it

your hands are raw with scraping
the sharp bark, the thorns
of this succulent tree
Pick, pick, pick
this harvest is a failure
the juice runs down your cheekbones
like sweat or tears

2.

She is the one you call sister
you blaze like lightning about the room
flicker around her like fire
dazzle yourself in her wide eyes
listing her unfelt needs
thrusting the tenets of your life
into her hands

She moves through a world of India print
her body dappled
with softness, the paisley swells at her hip
walking the street in her cotton shift
buying fresh figs because you love them
photographing the ghetto because you took her there

Why are you crying dry up your tears
we are sisters
words fail you in the stare of her hunger
you hand her another book
scored by your pencil
you hand her a record
of two flutes in India reciting

3.

Late summer night the insects
fry in the yellowed lightglobe
your skin burns gold in its light
In this mirror, who are you? Dreams of the nunnery

with its discipline, the nursery
with its nurse, the hospital
where all the powerful ones are masked
the graveyard where you sit on the graves
of women who died in childbirth
and women who died at birth
Dreams of your sister's birth
your mother dying in childbirth over and over
not knowing how to stop
bearing you over and over

your mother dead and you unborn
your two hands grasping your head
drawing it down against the blade of life
your nerves the nerves of a midwife
learning her trade

1971

Dialogue

She sits with one hand poised against her head, the
other turning an old ring to the light
for hours our talk has beaten
like rain against the screens
a sense of August and heat-lightning
I get up, go to make tea, come back
we look at each other
then she says (and this is what I live through
over and over)—she says: *I do not know
if sex is an illusion*

*I do not know
who I was when I did those things
or who I said I was*

or whether I willed to feel
what I had read about
or who in fact was there with me
or whether I knew, even then
that there was doubt about these things

1972

Diving into the Wreck

First having read the book of myths,
and loaded the camera,
and checked the edge of the knife-blade,
I put on
the body-armor of black rubber
the absurd flippers
the grave and awkward mask.
I am having to do this
not like Cousteau with his
assiduous team
aboard the sun-flooded schooner
but here alone.

There is a ladder.
The ladder is always there
hanging innocently
close to the side of the schooner.
We know what it is for,
we who have used it.
Otherwise
it's a piece of maritime floss
some sundry equipment.

I go down.
Rung after rung and still
the oxygen immerses me

the blue light
the clear atoms
of our human air.
I go down.
My flippers cripple me,
I crawl like an insect down the ladder
and there is no one
to tell me when the ocean
will begin.

First the air is blue and then
it is bluer and then green and then
black I am blacking out and yet
my mask is powerful
it pumps my blood with power
the sea is another story
the sea is not a question of power
I have to learn alone
to turn my body without force
in the deep element.

And now: it is easy to forget
what I came for
among so many who have always
lived here
swaying their crenellated fans
between the reefs
and besides
you breathe differently down here.

I came to explore the wreck.
The words are purposes.
The words are maps.
I came to see the damage that was done
and the treasures that prevail.
I stroke the beam of my lamp
slowly along the flank
of something more permanent
than fish or weed

the thing I came for:
the wreck and not the story of the wreck
the thing itself and not the myth
the drowned face always staring
toward the sun
the evidence of damage
worn by salt and sway into this threadbare beauty
the ribs of the disaster
curving their assertion
among the tentative haunters.

This is the place.
And I am here, the mermaid whose dark hair
streams black, the merman in his armored body
We circle silently
about the wreck
we dive into the hold.
I am she: I am he

whose drowned face sleeps with open eyes
whose breasts still bear the stress
whose silver, copper, vermeil cargo lies
obscurely inside barrels
half-wedged and left to rot
we are the half-destroyed instruments
that once held to a course
the water-eaten log
the fouled compass

We are, I am, you are
by cowardice or courage
the one who find our way
back to this scene
carrying a knife, a camera
a book of myths
in which
our names do not appear.

1972

The Phenomenology of Anger

1. The freedom of the wholly mad
to smear & play with her madness
write with her fingers dipped in it
the length of a room

which is not, of course, the freedom
you have, walking on Broadway
to stop & turn back or go on
10 blocks; 20 blocks

but feels enviable maybe
to the compromised

curled in the placenta of the real
which was to feed & which is strangling her.

2. Trying to light a log that's lain in the damp
as long as this house has stood:
even with dry sticks I can't get started
even with thorns.
I twist last year into a knot of old headlines
—this rose won't bloom.

How does a pile of rags the machinist wiped his hands on
feel in its cupboard, hour upon hour?
Each day during the heat-wave
they took the temperature of the haymow.
I huddled fugitive
in the warm sweet simmer of the hay

muttering: *Come.*

3. Flat heartland of winter.
The moonmen come back from the moon
the firemen come out of the fire.
Time without a taste: time without decisions.

•

Self-hatred, a monotone in the mind.
The shallowness of a life lived in exile
even in the hot countries.
Cleaver, staring into a window full of knives.

4. White light splits the room.
Table. Window. Lampshade. You.

My hands, sticky in a new way.
Menstrual blood
seeming to leak from your side.

Will the judges try to tell me
which was the blood of whom?

5. Madness. Suicide. Murder.
Is there no way out but these?
The enemy, always just out of sight
snowshoeing the next forest, shrouded
in a snowy blur, abominable snowman
—at once the most destructive
and the most elusive being
gunning down the babies at My Lai
vanishing in the face of confrontation.

The prince of air and darkness
computing body counts, masturbating
in the factory
of facts.

6. Fantasies of murder: not enough:
to kill is to cut off from pain
but the killer goes on hurting

Not enough. When I dream of meeting
the enemy, this is my dream:

white acetylene
ripples from my body
effortlessly released

perfectly trained
on the true enemy

raking his body down to the thread
of existence
burning away his lie
leaving him in a new
world; a changed
man

7. I suddenly see the world
as no longer viable:
you are out there burning the crops
with some new sublimate
This morning you left the bed
we still share
and went out to spread impotence
upon the world

I hate you.
I hate the mask you wear, your eyes
assuming a depth
they do not possess, drawing me
into the grotto of your skull
the landscape of bone
I hate your words
they make me think of fake
revolutionary bills
crisp imitation parchment
they sell at battlefields.

Last night, in this room, weeping
I asked you: *what are you feeling?*
do you feel anything?

Now in the torsion of your body
as you defoliate the fields we lived from
I have your answer.

•

8. Dogeared earth. Wormeaten moon.
A pale cross-hatching of silver
lies like a wire screen on the black
water. All these phenomena
are temporary.

I would have loved to live in a world
of women and men gaily
in collusion with green leaves, stalks,
building mineral cities, transparent domes,
little huts of woven grass
each with its own pattern—
a conspiracy to coexist
with the Crab Nebula, the exploding
universe, the Mind—

9. *The only real love I have ever felt*
was for children and other women.
Everything else was lust, pity,
self-hatred, pity, lust.
This is a woman's confession.
Now, look again at the face
of Botticelli's Venus, Kali,
the Judith of Chartres
with her so-called smile.

10. how we are burning up our lives
testimony:
                the subway
                hurtling to Brooklyn
                her head on her knees
                asleep or drugged

la vía del tren subterráneo
es peligrosa

                many sleep
                the whole way
                others sit
                staring holes of fire into the air
                others plan rebellion:

night after night
awake in prison, my mind
licked at the mattress like a flame
till the cellblock went up roaring

Thoreau setting fire to the woods

Every act of becoming conscious
(it says here in this book)
is an unnatural act

1972

Translations

You show me the poems of some woman
my age, or younger
translated from your language

Certain words occur: *enemy, oven, sorrow*
enough to let me know
she's a woman of my time

obsessed

with Love, our subject:
we've trained it like ivy to our walls
baked it like bread in our ovens
worn it like lead on our ankles
watched it through binoculars as if
it were a helicopter
bringing food to our famine
or the satellite
of a hostile power

•

I begin to see that woman
doing things: stirring rice
ironing a skirt
typing a manuscript till dawn

trying to make a call
from a phonebooth

The phone rings unanswered
in a man's bedroom
she hears him telling someone else
Never mind. She'll get tired—
hears him telling her story to her sister

who becomes her enemy
and will in her own time
light her own way to sorrow

ignorant of the fact this way of grief
is shared, unnecessary
and political

1972

Song

You're wondering if I'm lonely:
OK then, yes, I'm lonely
as a plane rides lonely and level
on its radio beam, aiming
across the Rockies
for the blue-strung aisles
of an airfield on the ocean

You want to ask, am I lonely?
Well, of course, lonely

as a woman driving across country
day after day, leaving behind
mile after mile
little towns she might have stopped
and lived and died in, lonely

If I'm lonely
it must be the loneliness
of waking first, of breathing
dawn's first cold breath on the city
of being the one awake
in a house wrapped in sleep

If I'm lonely
it's with the rowboat ice-fast on the shore
in the last red light of the year
that knows what it is, that knows it's neither
ice nor mud nor winter light
but wood, with a gift for burning

1971

The Ninth Symphony of Beethoven
Understood at Last as a Sexual Message

A man in terror of impotence
or infertility, not knowing the difference
a man trying to tell something
howling from the climacteric
music of the entirely
isolated soul
yelling at Joy from the tunnel of the ego
music without the ghost
of another person in it, music

trying to tell something the man
does not want out, would keep if he could
gagged and bound and flogged with chords of Joy
where everything is silence and the
beating of a bloody fist upon
a splintered table

1972

Rape

There is a cop who is both prowler and father:
he comes from your block, grew up with your brothers,
had certain ideals.
You hardly know him in his boots and silver badge,
on horseback, one hand touching his gun.

You hardly know him but you have to get to know him:
he has access to machinery that could kill you.
He and his stallion clop like warlords among the trash,
his ideals stand in the air, a frozen cloud
from between his unsmiling lips.

And so, when the time comes, you have to turn to him,
the maniac's sperm still greasing your thighs,
your mind whirling like crazy. You have to confess
to him, you are guilty of the crime
of having been forced.

And you see his blue eyes, the blue eyes of all the family
whom you used to know, grow narrow and glisten,
his hand types out the details
and he wants them all
but the hysteria in your voice pleases him best.

You hardly know him but now he thinks he knows you:
he has taken down your worst moment

on a machine and filed it in a file.
He knows, or thinks he knows, how much you imagined;
he knows, or thinks he knows, what you secretly wanted.

He has access to machinery that could get you put away;
and if, in the sickening light of the precinct,
and if, in the sickening light of the precinct,
your details sound like a portrait of your confessor,
will you swallow, will you deny them, will you lie your way home?

1972

Burning Oneself In

In a bookstore on the East Side
I read a veteran's testimony:

the running down, for no reason,
of an old woman in South Vietnam
by a U.S. Army truck

The heat-wave is over
Lifeless, sunny, the East Side
rests under its awnings

Another summer
The flames go on feeding

and a dull heat permeates the ground
of the mind, the burn has settled in
as if it had no more question

of its right to go on devouring
the rest of a lifetime,
the rest of history

Pieces of information, like this one
blow onto the heap

•

they keep it fed, whether we will it or not,
another summer, and another
of suffering quietly

in bookstores, in the parks
however we may scream we are
suffering quietly

1972

Burning Oneself Out

—for E.K.

We can look into the stove tonight
as into a mirror, yes,

the serrated log, the yellow-blue
gaseous core

the crimson-flittered grey ash, yes,
I know inside my eyelids
and underneath my skin

Time takes hold of us like a draft
upward, drawing at the heats
in the belly, in the brain

You told me of setting your hand
into the print of a long-dead Indian
and for a moment, I knew that hand,

that print, that rock,
that sun producing powerful dreams
A word can do this

•

or, as tonight, the mirror of the fire
of my mind, burning as if it could go on
burning itself, burning down

feeding on everything
till there is nothing in life
that has not fed that fire

1972

For a Sister

*Natalya Gorbanevskaya, two years
incarcerated in a Soviet penal mental asylum
for her political activism; and others.*

I trust none of them. Only my existence
thrown out in the world like a towchain
battered and twisted in many chance connections,
being pulled this way, pulling in that.

I have to steal the sense of dust on your floor,
milk souring in your pantry
after they came and took you.
I'm forced to guess at the look you threw backward.

A few paragraphs in the papers,
allowing for printers' errors, wilful omissions,
the trained violence of doctors.
I don't trust them, but I'm learning how to use them.

Little by little out of the blurred conjectures
your face clears, a sunken marble
slowly cranked up from underwater.
I feel the ropes straining under their load of despair.

They searched you for contraband, they made their notations.
A look of intelligence could get you twenty years.
Better to trace nonexistent circles with your finger,
try to imitate the smile of the permanently dulled.

My images. This metaphor for what happens.
A geranium in flames on a green cloth
becomes yours. You, coming home after years
to light the stove, get out the typewriter and begin again. Your story.

1972

From a Survivor

The pact that we made was the ordinary pact
of men & women in those days

I don't know who we thought we were
that our personalities
could resist the failures of the race

Lucky or unlucky, we didn't know
the race had failures of that order
and that we were going to share them

Like everybody else, we thought of ourselves as special

Your body is as vivid to me
as it ever was: even more

since my feeling for it is clearer:
I know what it could and could not do

it is no longer
the body of a god
or anything with power over my life

•

Next year it would have been 20 years
and you are wastefully dead
who might have made the leap
we talked, too late, of making

which I live now
not as a leap
but a succession of brief, amazing movements

each one making possible the next

1972

For the Dead

I dreamed I called you on the telephone
to say: *Be kinder to yourself*
but you were sick and would not answer

The waste of my love goes on this way
trying to save you from yourself

I have always wondered about the leftover
energy, water rushing down a hill
long after the rains have stopped

or the fire you want to go to bed from
but cannot leave, burning-down but not burnt-down
the red coals more extreme, more curious
in their flashing and dying
than you wish they were
sitting there long after midnight

1972

August

Two horses in yellow light
eating windfall apples under a tree

as summer tears apart   milkweeds stagger
and grasses grow more ragged

They say there are ions in the sun
neutralizing magnetic fields on earth

Some way to explain
what this week has been, and the one before it!

If I am flesh sunning on rock
if I am brain burning in fluorescent light

if I am dream like a wire with fire
throbbing along it

if I am death to man
I have to know it

His mind is too simple, I cannot go on
sharing his nightmares

My own are becoming clearer, they open
into prehistory

which looks like a village lit with blood
where all the fathers are crying: *My son is mine!*

1972

Meditations for a Savage Child

*The prose passages are from J.-M. Itard's ac-
count of* The Wild Boy of Aveyron, *as translated
by G. and M. Humphrey.*

*There was a profound indifference to the objects of our plea-
sures and of our fictitious needs; there was still . . . so intense a
passion for the freedom of the fields . . . that he would certainly
have escaped into the forest had not the most rigid precautions been
taken . . .*

In their own way, by their own lights
they tried to care for you
tried to teach you to care
for objects of their caring:

        glossed oak planks, glass
        whirled in a fire
        to impossible thinness

to teach you names
for things
you did not need

        muslin shirred against the sun
        linen on a sack of feathers
        locks, keys
        boxes with coins inside

they tried to make you feel
the importance of

        a piece of cowhide
        sewn around a bundle
        of leaves impressed with signs

●

to teach you language:
the thread their lives
were strung on

II

*When considered from a more general and philosophic point of
view, these scars bear witness . . . against the feebleness and in-
sufficiency of man when left entirely to himself, and in favor of the
resources of nature which . . . work openly to repair and conserve
that which she tends secretly to impair and destroy.*

I keep thinking about the lesson of the human ear
which stands for music, which stands for balance—
or the cat's ear which I can study better
the whorls and ridges exposed
It seems a hint dropped about the inside of the skull
which I cannot see
lobe, zone, that part of the brain
which is pure survival

The most primitive part
I go back into at night
pushing the leathern curtain
with naked fingers
then
with naked body

There where every wound is registered
as scar tissue

A cave of scars!
ancient, archaic wallpaper
built up, layer on layer
from the earliest, dream-white
to yesterday's, a red-black scrawl
a red mouth slowly closing

•

Go back so far there is another language
go back far enough the language
is no longer personal

these scars bear witness
but whether to repair
or to destruction
I no longer know

III

*It is true that there is visible on the throat a very extended scar
which might throw some doubt upon the soundness of the underly-
ing parts if one were not reassured by the appearance of the
scar . . .*

When I try to speak
my throat is cut
and, it seems, by his hand

The sounds I make are prehuman, radical
the telephone is always
ripped-out

and he sleeps on
Yet always the tissue
grows over, white as silk

hardly a blemish
maybe a hieroglyph for scream

Child, no wonder you never wholly
trusted your keepers

IV

*A hand with the will rather than the habit of crime had wished
to make an attempt on the life of this child . . . left for dead in
the woods, he will have owed the prompt recovery of his wound to
the help of nature alone.*

•

In the 18th century infanticide
reaches epidemic proportions:
old prints attest to it: starving mothers
smothering babies in sleep
abandoning newborns in sleet
on the poorhouse steps
gin-blurred, setting fire to the room

I keep thinking of the flights we used to take
on the grapevine across the gully
littered with beer-bottles where dragonflies flashed
we were 10, 11 years old
wild little girls with boyish bodies
flying over the moist
shadow-mottled earth
till they warned us to stay away from there

Later they pointed out
the venetian blinds
of the abortionist's house
we shivered

Men can do things to you
was all they said

V

And finally, my Lord, looking at this long experiment . . . whether it be considered as the methodical education of a savage or as no more than the physical and moral treatment of one of those creatures ill-favored by nature, rejected by society and abandoned by medicine, the care that has been taken and ought still to be taken of him, the changes that have taken place, and those that can be hoped for, the voice of humanity, the interest inspired by such a desertion and a destiny so strange—all these things recommend this extraordinary young man to the attention of scientists, to the solicitude of administrators, and to the protection of the government.

  1. The doctor in "Uncle Vanya":
     They will call us fools,

blind, ignorant, they will
despise us

devourers of the forest
leaving teeth of metal in every tree
so the tree can neither grow
nor be cut for lumber

Does the primeval forest
weep
for its devourers

does nature mourn
our existence

is the child with arms
burnt to the flesh of its sides
weeping eyelessly for man

2. At the end of the distinguished doctor's
lecture
a young woman raises her hand:

You have the power
in your hands, you control our lives—
why do you want our pity too?

Why are men afraid
why do you pity yourselves
why do the administrators

lack solicitude, the government
refuse protection,

why should the wild child
weep for the scientists

why

1972

Poems
1950-1974

The Prisoners

Enclosed in this disturbing mutual wood,
Wounded alike by thorns of the same tree,
We seek in hopeless war each others' blood
Though suffering in one identity.
Each to the other prey and huntsman known,
Still driven together, lonelier than alone.

Strange mating of the loser and the lost!
With faces stiff as mourners', we intrude
Forever on the one each turns from most,
Each wandering in a double solitude.
The unpurged ghosts of passion bound by pride
Who wake in isolation, side by side.

1950

Night

The motes that still disturbed her lidded calm
Were these: the tick and whisper of a shade
Against the sill; a cobweb-film that hung
Aslant a corner moulding, too elusive
For any but the gaze of straitened eyes;
The nimbus of the night-lamp, where a moth
Uneasily explored the edge of light
Through hours of fractured darkness. She alone
Knew that the room contained these things; she lay
Hearing the almost imperceptible sound
(As if a live thing shivered behind the curtains)
Watching the thread that frayed in gusts of air

187

More delicate than her breathing, or by night
Sharing a moth's perplexity at light
Too frail to drive out dark: minutiae
Held in the vise of sense about to die.

1950

The House at the Cascades

All changed now through neglect. The steps dismantled
By infantries of ants, by roots and storms,
The pillars tugged by vines, the porte-cochère
A passageway for winds, the solemn porches
Warped into caricatures.
                              We came at evening
After the rain, when every drunken leaf
Was straining, swelling in a riot of green.
Only the house was dying in all that life,
As if a triumph of emerald energy
Had fixed its mouth upon the walls and stones.
The tamest shrub remembered anarchy
And joined in appetite with the demagogue weed
That springs where order falls; together there
They stormed the defenseless handiwork of man
Whose empire wars against him when he turns
A moment from the yoke. So, turning back,
He sees his rooftree fall to furious green,
His yard despoiled, and out of innocent noon
The insect-cloud like thunder on the land.

1951

At the Jewish New Year

For more than five thousand years
This calm September day
With yellow in the leaf
Has lain in the kernel of Time
While the world outside the walls
Has had its turbulent say
And history like a long
Snake has crawled on its way
And is crawling onward still.
And we have little to tell
On this or any feast
Except of the terrible past.
Five thousand years are cast
Down before the wondering child
Who must expiate them all.

Some of us have replied
In the bitterness of youth
Or the qualms of middle-age:
"If Time is unsatisfied,
And all our fathers have suffered
Can never be enough,
Why, then, we choose to forget.
Let our forgetting begin
With those age-old arguments
In which their minds were wound
Like musty phylacteries;
And we choose to forget as well
Those cherished histories
That made our old men fond,
And already are strange to us.

•

"Or let us, being today
Too rational to cry out,
Or trample underfoot
What after all preserves
A certain savor yet—
Though torn up by the roots—
Let us make our compromise
With the terror and the guilt
And view as curious relics
Once found in daily use
The mythology, the names
That, however Time has corrupted
Their ancient purity
Still burn like yellow flames,
But their fire is not for us."

And yet, however we choose
To deny or to remember,
Though on the calendars
We wake and suffer by,
This day is merely one
Of thirty in September—
In the kernel of the mind
The new year must renew
This day, as for our kind
Over five thousand years,
The task of being ourselves.
Whatever we strain to forget,
Our memory must be long.

May the taste of honey linger
Under the bitterest tongue.

1955

Moving in Winter

Their life, collapsed like unplayed cards,
is carried piecemeal through the snow:
Headboard and footboard now, the bed
where she has lain desiring him
where overhead his sleep will build
its canopy to smother her once more;
their table, by four elbows worn
evening after evening while the wax runs down;
mirrors grey with reflecting them,
bureaus coffining from the cold
things that can shuffle in a drawer,
carpets rolled up around those echoes
which, shaken out, take wing and breed
new altercations, the old silences.

1957

To Judith, Taking Leave

—for J.H.

Dull-headed, with dull fingers
I patch once more
the pale brown envelope
still showing under ink scratches
the letterhead of MIND.
A chorus of old postmarks
echoes across its face.
It looks so frail
to send so far

and I should tear it across
mindlessly
and find another.
But I'm tired, can't endure
a single new motion
or room or object,
so I cling to this too
as if your tallness moving
against the rainlight
in an Amsterdam flat
might be held awhile
by a handwritten label
or a battered envelope
from your desk.

Once somewhere else
I shan't talk of you
as a singular event
or a beautiful thing I saw
though both are true.
I shan't falsify you
through praising and describing
as I shall other
things I have loved
almost as much.
There in Amsterdam
you'll be living as I
have seen you live
and as I've never seen you.
And I can trust
no plane to bring you
my life out there
in turbid America—
my own life, lived against
facts I keep there.

It wasn't literacy—
the right to read MIND—
or suffrage—to vote

for the lesser of two
evils—that were
the great gains, I see now,
when I think of all those women
who suffered ridicule
for us.
But this little piece of ground,
Judith! that two women
in love to the nerves' limit
with two men—
shared out in pieces
to men, children, memories
so different and so draining—
should think it possible
now for the first time
perhaps, to love each other
neither as fellow-victims
nor as a temporary
shadow of something better.
Still shared-out as we are,
lovers, poets, warmers
of men and children
against our flesh, not knowing
from day to day
what we'll fling out on the water
or what pick up
there at the tide's lip,
often tired, as I'm tired now
from sheer distances of soul
we have in one day to cover—
still to get here
to this little spur or headland
and feel now free enough
to leave our weapons somewhere
else—such are the secret
outcomes of revolution!
that two women can meet
no longer as cramped sharers
of a bitter mutual secret

but as two eyes in one brow
receiving at one moment
the rainbow of the world.

1962

Roots

—for M.L.

Evenings seem endless, now
dark tugs at our sky
harder and earlier
and milkweeds swell to bursting . . .
now in my transatlantic eye
you stand on your terrace
a scarf on your head and in your hands
dead stalks of golden-glow

and now it's for you,
not myself, I shiver
hearing glass doors rattle
at your back, the rustling cough
of a dry clematis vine
your love and toil trained up the walls
of a rented house.

All those roots, Margo!
Didn't you start each slip between your breasts,
each dry seed, carrying some
across frontiers, knotted
into your handkerchief,
haven't you seen your tears
glisten in narrow trenches
where rooted cuttings grope for life?

●

You, frailer than you look,
long back, long stride, blond hair
coiled up over straight shoulders—
I hear in your ear the wind
lashing in wet from the North Sea
slamming the dahlias flat.
All your work violated
every autumn, every turn of the wrist
guiding the trowel: mocked.
Sleet on brown fibers,
black wilt eating your harvest,
a clean sweep, and you the loser . . .

or is this after all
the liberation your hands fend off
and your eyes implore
when you dream of sudden death
or of beginning anew,
a girl of seventeen, the war just over,
and all the gardens
to dig again?

1963

The Parting: II

White morning flows into the mirror.
Her eye, still old with sleep,
meets itself like a sister.

How they slept last night,
the dream that caged them back to back,
was nothing new.

Last words, tears, most often

come wrapped as the everyday
familiar failure.

Now, pulling the comb slowly
through her loosened hair
she tries to find the parting;

it must come out after all:
hidden in all that tangle
there is a way.

1963

White Night

—from the Yiddish of Kadia Molodovsky

White night, my painful joy,
your light is brighter than the dawn.
A white ship is sailing from East Broadway
where I see no sail by day.

A quiet star hands me a ticket
open for all the seas.
I put on my time-worn jacket
and entrust myself to the night.

Where are you taking me, ship?
Who charted us on this course?
The hieroglyphs of the map escape me,
and the arrows of your compass.

I am the one who sees and does not see.
I go along on your deck of secrets,
squeeze shut my baggage on the wreath of sorrows
from all my plucked-out homes.

•

—Pack in all my blackened pots,
their split lids, the chipped crockeries,
pack in my chaos with its gold-encrusted buttons
since chaos will always be in fashion.

—Pack the letters stamped *Unknown at This Address*—
vanished addresses that sear my eyes,
postmarked with more than years and days;
sucked into my bones and marrow.

—Pack up my shadow that weighs more than my body,
that comes along with its endless exhortations.
Weekdays or holidays, time of flowers or withering,
my shadow is with me, muttering its troubles.

Find me a place of honey cakes and sweetness
where angels and children picnic together
(this is the dream I love best of all),
Where the sacred wine fizzes in bottles.

Let me have one sip, here on East Broadway,
for the sake of those old Jews crying in the dark.
I cry my heretic's tears with them,
their sobbing is my sobbing.

I'm a difficult passenger, my ship
is packed with the heavy horns, the *shofars* of grief.
Tighten the sails of night as far as you can,
for the daylight cannot carry me.

Take me somewhere to a place of rest,
of goats in belled hats playing on trombones—
to the Almighty's fresh white sheets
where the hunter's shadow cannot fall.

Take me . . . Yes, take me . . . But you know best
where the sea calmly opens its blue road.
I'm wearier than your oldest tower;
somewhere I've left my heart aside.

Tear Gas

(October 12, 1969: reports of the tear-gassing of demonstrators
protesting the treatment of G.I. prisoners in the stockade at
Fort Dix, New Jersey)

This is how it feels to do something you are afraid of.
That they are afraid of.

   (Would it have been different at Fort Dix, beginning
to feel the full volume of tears in you, the measure
of all you have in you to shed, all you have held
back from false pride, false indifference, false
courage

beginning to weep as you weep peeling onions, but
endlessly, for the rest of time, tears of chemistry,
tears of catalyst, tears of rage, tears for yourself,
tears for the tortured men in the stockade and for
their torturers

tears of fear, of the child stepping into the adult
field of force, the woman stepping into the male field
of violence, tears of relief, that your body was here,
you had done it, every last refusal was over)

Here in this house my tears are running wild
in this Vermont of india-madras-colored leaves, of cesspool-
    stricken brooks, of violence licking at old people and
    children
and I am afraid
of the language in my head
I am alone, alone with language
and without meaning
coming back to something written years ago:
our words misunderstand us

    ●

wanting a word that will shed itself like a tear
onto the page
leaving its stain

Trying every key in the bunch to get the door even ajar
not knowing whether it's locked or simply jammed from long disuse
trying the keys over and over then throwing the bunch away
staring around for an axe
wondering if the world can be changed like this
if a life can be changed like this

It wasn't completeness I wanted
(the old ideas of a revolution that could be foretold, and once
        arrived at would give us ourselves and each other)
I stopped listening long ago to their descriptions
of the good society

The will to change begins in the body not in the mind
My politics is in my body, accruing and expanding with every
        act of resistance and each of my failures
Locked in the closet at 4 years old I beat the wall with my body
that act is in me still

No, not completeness:
but I needed a way of saying
(this is what they are afraid of)
that could deal with these fragments
I needed to touch you
with a hand, a body
but also with words
I need a language to hear myself with
to see myself in
a language like pigment released on the board
blood-black, sexual green, reds
veined with contradictions
bursting under pressure from the tube
staining the old grain of the wood
like sperm or tears
but this is not what I mean

these images are not what I mean
(I am afraid.)
I mean that I want you to answer me
when I speak badly
that I love you, that we are in danger
that she wants to have your child, that I want us to have mercy
    on each other
that I want to take her hand
that I see you changing
that it was change I loved in you
when I thought I loved completeness
that things I have said which in a few years will be forgotten
matter more to me than this or any poem
and I want you to listen
when I speak badly
not in poems but in tears
not my best but my worst
that these repetitions are beating their way
toward a place where we can no longer be together
where my body no longer will demonstrate outside your stockade
and wheeling through its blind tears will make for the open air
of another kind of action

(I am afraid.)
It's not the worst way to live.

1969

Dien Bien Phu

A nurse on the battlefield
wounded herself, but working

    dreams
        that each man she touches
        is a human grenade

an anti-personnel weapon
that can explode in her arms

How long
can she go on like this
putting mercy
ahead of survival

She is walking
in a white dress stained
with earth and blood

down a road lined
with fields long
given up   blasted

cemeteries of one name
or two

A hand
juts out like barbed wire
it is terribly alone

if she takes it
will it slash her wrists again

if she passes it by

will she turn into a case
of shell-shock, eyes
glazed forever on the

blank chart of
amnesia

1973

Essential Resources

I don't know
how late it is. I'm writing
with a chewed blunted lead
under a bridge while snow blankets the city
or with a greasy ballpoint
the nurse left
in a ward of amnesiacs who can be trusted
not to take notes

You talk of a film we could make
with women's faces naked
of make-up, the mist of sweat
on a forehead, lips dry
the little bloodspot from a coldsore

I know the inmates are encouraged
to express themselves
I'm wondering how

I long to create something
that can't be used to keep us passive:
I want to write
a script about plumbing, how every pipe
is joined
to every other

the wash of pure water and sewage
side by side

or about the electrical system
a study of the sources of energy
till in the final shot
the whole screen goes dark
and the keepers of order are screaming

●

I forget
what year it is. I am thinking
of films we have made but cannot show
yet, films of the mind unfolding
and our faces, still young
sweated with desire and
premature clarity

1973

Blood-Sister

—for Cynthia

Shoring up the ocean. A railroad track
ran close to the coast for miles
through the potato-fields, bringing us
to summer. Weeds blur the ties,
sludge clots the beaches.

During the war, the shells we found—
salmon-and-silver coins
sand dollars dripping sand
like dust. We were dressed
in navy dotted-swiss dresses in the train
not to show the soot. Like dolls
we sat with our dolls in the station.

When did we begin to dress ourselves?

Now I'm wearing jeans spider-webbed
with creases, a black sweater bought years ago
worn almost daily since
the ocean has undergone a tracheotomy
and lost its resonance
you wear a jersey the color of

Navaho turquoise and sand
you are holding a naked baby girl
she laughs into your eyes
we sit at your table drinking coffee
light flashes off unwashed sheetglass
you are more beautiful than you have ever been

we talk of destruction and creation
ice fits itself around each twig of the lilac
like a fist of law and order
your imagination burns like a bulb in the frozen soil
the fierce shoots knock
at the roof of waiting

when summer comes the ocean may be closed for good
we will turn
to the desert
where survival
takes naked and fiery forms

1973

The Wave

—for J.B.

To give you back this wave
I would have to give back
the black
spaces

fretted with film of spray,
darker and deeper than the mind
they are emblems of

Not only the creator fury
of the whitest churn

the caldron of all life
but the blankness underlying

Thinking of the sea I think of light
lacing, lancing the water
the blue knife of a radiant consciousness
bent by the waves of vision as it pierces
to the deepest grotto

And I think of those lives we tried to live
in our globed helmets, self-enclosed
bodies self-illumined gliding
safe from the turbulence

and how, miraculously, we failed

1973

Re-forming the Crystal

I am trying to imagine
how it feels to you
to want a woman

trying to hallucinate
desire
centered in a cock
focused like a burning-glass

desire without discrimination:
to want a woman like a fix

Desire: yes: the sudden knowledge, like coming out of 'flu, that the
body is sexual. Walking in the streets with that knowledge. That
evening in the plane from Pittsburgh, fantasizing going to meet
you. Walking through the airport blazing with energy and joy. But

knowing all along that you were not the source of that energy and joy; you were a man, a stranger, a name, a voice on the telephone, a friend; this desire was mine, this energy my energy; it could be used a hundred ways, and going to meet you could be one of them.

> Tonight is a different kind of night.
> I sit in the car, racing the engine,
> calculating the thinness of the ice.
> In my head I am already threading the beltways
> that rim this city,
> all the old roads that used to wander the country
> having been lost.
> Tonight I understand
> my photo on the license is not me,
> my
> name on the marriage-contract was not mine.
> If I remind you of my father's favorite daughter,
> look again. The woman
> I needed to call my mother
> was silenced before I was born.

Tonight if the battery charges I want to take the car out on sheet-ice; I want to understand my fear both of the machine and of the accidents of nature. My desire for you is not trivial; I can compare it with the greatest of those accidents. But the energy it draws on might lead to racing a cold engine, cracking the frozen spiderweb, parachuting into the field of a poem wired with danger, or to a trip through gorges and canyons, into the cratered night of female memory, where delicately and with intense care the chieftainess inscribes upon the ribs of the volcano the name of the one she has chosen.

1973

White Night

Light at a window. Someone up
at this snail-still hour.
We who work this way have often worked
in solitude. I've had to guess at her
sewing her skin together as I sew mine
though
with a different
stitch.

Dawn after dawn, this neighbor
burns like a candle
dragging her bedspread through the dark house
to her dark bed
her head
full of runes, syllables, refrains,
this accurate dreamer

sleepwalks the kitchen
like a white moth,
an elephant, a guilt.
Somebody tried to put her
to rest under an afghan
knitted with wools the color of grass and blood

but she has risen. Her lamplight
licks at the icy panes
and melts into the dawn.
They will never prevent her
who sleep the stone sleep of the past,
the sleep of the drugged.
One crystal second, I flash

•

an eye across the cold
unwrapping of light between us
into her darkness-lancing eye
—that's all. Dawn is the test, the agony
but we were meant to see it:
After this, we may sleep, my sister,
while the flames rise higher and higher, we can sleep.

1974

Amnesia

I almost trust myself to know
when we're getting to that scene—
call it the snow-scene in *Citizen Kane:*

the mother handing over her son
the earliest American dream
shot in a black-and-white

where every flake of snow
is incandescent
with its own burden, adding-

up, always adding-up to the
cold blur of the past
But first there is the picture of the past

simple and pitiless as the deed
truly was
the putting-away of a childish thing

Becoming a man means leaving
someone, or something—
still, why

●

must the snow-scene blot itself out
the flakes come down so fast
so heavy, so unrevealing

over the something that gets left behind?

1974

For L.G.: Unseen for Twenty Years

A blue-grained line circles a fragment of the mind
drawn in ancient crayon:
out of the blue, your tightstrung smile—

often in the first snow
that even here smells only of itself
even on this Broadway limped by cripples
and the self-despising
Still, in that smell, another snow,
another world: we're walking
grey boulevards traced with white
in Paris, the early 'fifties
of invincible ignorance:

or, a cold spring:
I clasp your hips on the bike
shearing the empty plain in March
teeth gritted in the wind
searching for Chartres:
we doze
in the boat-train

we who were friends and thought
women and men should be lovers

●

Your face: taut as a mask of wires, a fencer's mask
half-turned away, the one night, walking
the City of Love, so cold
we warmed our nerves with wine
at every all-night café
to keep on walking, talking
Your words have drifted back for twenty years:

I have to tell you—maybe I'm not a man—
I can't do it with women—but I'd like
to hold you, to know what it's like
to sleep and wake together—

the one night in all our weeks of talk
you talked of fear
                              I wonder

what words of mine drift back to you?
Something like:
                    But you're a man, I know it—
the swiftness of your mind is masculine—?

—some set-piece I'd learned to embroider
in my woman's education
while the needle scarred my hand?

Of course, you're a man. I like you. What else could you be?
what else, what else,
what bloody else . . .

Given the cruelty of our times and customs,
maybe you hate these memories,
the ignorance, the innocence we shared:
maybe you cruise the SoHo cocktail parties
the Vancouver bar-scene
stalking yourself as I can see you still:
young, tense, amorphous, longing—

        •

maybe you live out your double life
in the Berkeley hills, with a wife
who stuns her mind into indifference
with Scotch and saunas
while you arrange your own humiliations
downtown

(and, yes, I've played my scenes
of favorite daughter, child-bride, token woman, muse
listening now and then
as a drunken poet muttered into my hair:
I can't make it with women I admire—)

maybe you've found or fought
through to a kind of faithfulness
in the strange coexistence
of two of any gender

But we were talking in 1952
of the fear of being cripples in a world
of perfect women and men:
we were the givens and the stake
and we did badly

and, dear heart, I know, had a lover gestured
you'd have left me
for a man, as I left you,
as we left each other, seeking the love of men.

1974

From an Old House in America

1.

Deliberately, long ago
the carcasses

of old bugs crumbled
into the rut of the window

and we started sleeping here
Fresh June bugs batter this June's

screens, June-lightning batters
the spiderweb

I sweep the wood-dust
from the wood-box

the snout of the vacuum cleaner
sucks the past away

2.

Other lives were lived here:
mostly un-articulate

yet someone left her creamy signature
in the trail of rusticated

narcissus straggling up
through meadowgrass and vetch

Families breathed close
boxed-in from the cold

hard times, short growing season
the old rainwater cistern

●

hulks in the cellar

3.

Like turning through the contents of a drawer:
these rusted screws, this empty vial

useless, this box of watercolor paints
dried to insolubility—

but this—
this pack of cards with no card missing

still playable
and three good fuses

and this toy: a little truck
scarred red, yet all its wheels still turn

The humble tenacity of things
waiting for people, waiting for months, for years

4.

Often rebuked, yet always back returning
I place my hand on the hand

of the dead, invisible palm-print
on the doorframe

spiked with daylilies, green leaves
catching in the screen door

or I read the backs of old postcards
curling from thumbtacks, winter and summer

fading through cobweb-tinted panes—
white church in Norway

Dutch hyacinths bleeding azure
red beach on Corsica

•

set-pieces of the world
stuck to this house of plank

I flash on wife and husband
embattled, in the years

that dried, dim ink was wet
those signatures

5.

If they call me man-hater, you
would have known it for a lie

but the *you* I want to speak to
has become your death

If I dream of you these days
I know my dreams are mine and not of you

yet something hangs between us
older and stranger than ourselves

like a translucent curtain, a sheet of water
a dusty window

the irreducible, incomplete connection
between the dead and living

or between man and woman in this
savagely fathered and unmothered world

6.

The other side of a translucent
curtain, a sheet of water

a dusty window, Non-being
utters its flat tones

the speech of an actor learning his lines
phonetically

•

the final autistic statement
of the self-destroyer

All my energy reaches out tonight
to comprehend a miracle beyond

raising the dead: the undead to watch
back on the road of birth

7.

I am an American woman:
I turn that over

like a leaf pressed in a book
I stop and look up from

into the coals of the stove
or the black square of the window

Foot-slogging through the Bering Strait
jumping from the *Arbella* to my death

chained to the corpse beside me
I feel my pains begin

I am washed up on this continent
shipped here to be fruitful

my body a hollow ship
bearing sons to the wilderness

sons who ride away
on horseback, daughters

whose juices drain like mine
into the *arroyo* of stillbirths, massacres

Hanged as witches, sold as breeding-wenches
my sisters leave me

●

I am not the wheatfield
nor the virgin forest

I never chose this place
yet I am of it now

In my decent collar, in the daguerrotype
I pierce its legend with my look

my hands wring the necks of prairie chickens
I am used to blood

When the men hit the hobo track
I stay on with the children

my power is brief and local
but I know my power

I have lived in isolation
from other women, so much

in the mining camps, the first cities
the Great Plains winters

Most of the time, in my sex, I was alone

8.

Tonight in this northeast kingdom
striated iris stand in a jar with daisies

the porcupine gnaws in the shed
fireflies beat and simmer

caterpillars begin again
their long, innocent climb

the length of leaves of burdock
or webbing of a garden chair

•

plain and ordinary things
speak softly

the light square on old wallpaper
where a poster has fallen down

Robert Indiana's LOVE
leftover of a decade

9.

I do not want to simplify
Or: I would simplify

by naming the complexity
It was made over-simple all along

the separation of powers
the allotment of sufferings

her spine cracking in labor
his plow driving across the Indian graves

her hand unconscious on the cradle, her mind
with the wild geese

his mother-hatred driving him
into exile from the earth

the refugee couple with their cardboard luggage
standing on the ramshackle landing-stage

he with fingers frozen around his Law
she with her down quilt sewn through iron nights

—the weight of the old world, plucked
drags after them, a random feather-bed

•

10.

Her children dead of diphtheria, she
set herself on fire with kerosene

(O Lord I was unworthy
Thou didst find me out)

she left the kitchen scrubbed
down to the marrow of its boards

"The penalty for barrenness
is emptiness

my punishment is my crime
what I have failed to do, is me . . ."

—Another month without a show
and this the seventh year

O Father let this thing pass out of me
I swear to You

I will live for the others, asking nothing
I will ask nothing, ever, for myself

11.

Out back of this old house
datura tangles with a gentler weed

its spiked pods smelling
of bad dreams and death

I reach through the dark, groping
past spines of nightmare

to brush the leaves of sensuality
A dream of tenderness

●

wrestles with all I know of history
I cannot now lie down

with a man who fears my power
or reaches for me as for death

or with a lover who imagines
we are not in danger

12.

If it was lust that had defined us—
their lust and fear of our deep places

we have done our time
as faceless torsos licked by fire

we are in the open, on our way—
our counterparts

the pinyon jay, the small
gilt-winged insect

the Cessna throbbing level
the raven floating in the gorge

the rose and violet vulva of the earth
filling with darkness

yet deep within a single sparkle
of red, a human fire

and near and yet above the western planet
calmly biding her time

13.

They were the distractions, lust and fear
but are

themselves a key
Everything that can be used, will be:

the fathers in their ceremonies
the genital contests

the cleansing of blood from pubic hair
the placenta buried and guarded

their terror of blinding
by the look of her who bore them

If you do not believe
that fear and hatred

read the lesson again
in the old dialect

14.

But can't you see me as a human being
he said

What is a human being
she said

I try to understand
he said

what will you undertake
she said

will you punish me for history
he said

what will you undertake
she said

do you believe in collective guilt
he said

●

let me look in your eyes
she said

15.

Who is here. The Erinyes.
One to sit in judgment.

One to speak tenderness.
One to inscribe the verdict on the canyon wall.

If you have not confessed
the damage

if you have not recognized
the Mother of reparations

if you have not come to terms
with the women in the mirror

if you have not come to terms
with the inscription

the terms of the ordeal
the discipline   the verdict

if still you are on your way
still She awaits your coming

16.

"Such women are dangerous
to the order of things"

and yes, we will be dangerous
to ourselves

groping through spines of nightmare
(*datura* tangling with a simpler herb)

●

because the line dividing
lucidity from darkness

is yet to be marked out

Isolation, the dream
of the frontier woman

leveling her rifle along
the homestead fence

still snares our pride
—a suicidal leaf

laid under the burning-glass
in the sun's eye

Any woman's death diminishes me

1974

From

The Dream of a Common Language

1978

Power

Living   in the earth-deposits   of our history

Today a backhoe divulged   out of a crumbling flank of earth
one bottle   amber   perfect   a hundred-year-old
cure for fever   or melancholy   a tonic
for living on this earth   in the winters of this climate

Today I was reading about Marie Curie:
she must have known she suffered   from radiation sickness
her body bombarded for years   by the element
she had purified
It seems she denied to the end
the source of the cataracts on her eyes
the cracked and suppurating skin   of her finger-ends
till she could no longer hold   a test-tube or a pencil

She died   a famous woman   denying
her wounds
denying
her wounds   came   from the same source as her power

1974

Phantasia for Elvira Shatayev

> *Leader of a women's climbing team, all of whom died in a*
> *storm on Lenin Peak, August 1974. Later, Shatayev's*
> *husband found and buried the bodies.*

The cold felt cold until our blood
grew colder   then the wind
died down and we slept

•   225

If in this sleep I speak
it's with a voice no longer personal
(I want to say   *with voices*)
When the wind tore   our breath from us at last
we had no need of words
For months   for years   each one of us
had felt her own *yes*   growing in her
slowly forming   as she stood at windows   waited
for trains   mended her rucksack   combed her hair
What we were to learn   was simply   what we had
up here   as out of all words   that *yes*   gathered
its forces   fused itself   and only just in time
to meet a *No* of no degrees
the black hole   sucking the world in

I feel you climbing toward me
your cleated bootsoles leaving   their geometric bite
colossally embossed   on microscopic crystals
as when I trailed you in the Caucasus
Now I am further
ahead   than either of us dreamed   anyone would be
I have become
the white snow packed like asphalt by the wind
the women I love   lightly flung   against the mountain
that blue sky
our frozen eyes unribboned   through the storm
we could have stitched that blueness   together   like a quilt

You come (I know this) with your love   your loss
strapped to your body   with your tape-recorder   camera
ice-pick   against advisement
to give us burial in the snow   and in your mind
While my body lies out here
flashing like a prism   into your eyes
how could you sleep   You climbed here for yourself
we climbed for ourselves

When you have buried us   told your story
ours does not end   we stream

into the unfinished   the unbegun
the possible
Every cell's core of heat   pulsed out of us
into the thin air   of the universe
the armature of rock beneath these snows
this mountain   which has taken   the imprint of our minds
through changes elemental and minute
as those we underwent
to bring each other here
choosing ourselves   each other   and this life
whose every breath   and grasp   and further foothold
is somewhere   still enacted   and continuing

In the diary I wrote: *Now we are ready*
and each of us knows it   I have never loved
like this   I have never seen
my own forces so taken up and shared
and given back
After the long training   the early sieges
we are moving almost effortlessly in our love

In the diary as the wind   began to tear
at the tents over us   I wrote:
We know now we have always been in danger
down in our separateness
and now up here together   but till now
we had not touched our strength

In the diary torn from my fingers I had written:
What does love mean
what does it mean   "to survive"
A cable of blue fire ropes our bodies
burning together in the snow   We will not live
to settle for less   We have dreamed of this
all of our lives

1974

Splittings

1.

My body opens over San Francisco like the day-
light raining down   each pore crying the change of light
I am not with her   I have been waking off and on
all night to that pain   not simply absence but
the presence of the past   destructive
to living here and now   Yet if I could instruct
myself, if we could learn to learn from pain
even as it grasps us   if the mind, the mind that lives
in this body could refuse   to let itself be crushed
in that grasp   it would loosen   Pain would have to stand
off from me and listen   its dark breath still on me
but the mind could begin to speak to pain
and pain would have to answer:

                              We are older now
we have met before   these are my hands before your eyes
my figure blotting out   all that is not mine
I am the pain of division   creator of divisions
it is I who blot your lover from you
and not the time-zones nor the miles
It is not separation calls me forth   but I
who am separation   And remember
I have no existence   apart from you

2.

I believe I am choosing something new
not to suffer uselessly   yet still to feel
Does the infant memorize the body of the mother
and create her in absence?   or simply cry
primordial loneliness?   does the bed of the stream
once diverted   mourning   remember wetness?

But we, we live so much in these
configurations of the past   I choose
to separate her   from my past we have not shared
I choose not to suffer uselessly
to detect primordial pain as it stalks toward me
flashing its bleak torch in my eyes   blotting out
her particular being   the details of her love
I will not be divided   from her or from myself
by myths of separation
while her mind and body in Manhattan are more with me
than the smell of eucalyptus coolly burning   on these hills

3.

The world tells me I am its creature
I am raked by eyes   brushed by hands
I want to crawl into her for refuge   lay my head
in the space   between her breast and shoulder
abnegating power for love
as women have done   or hiding
from power in her love   like a man
I refuse these givens   the splitting
between love and action   I am choosing
not to suffer uselessly   and not to use her
I choose to love   this time   for once
with all my intelligence

1974

Hunger

—for Audre Lorde

1.

A fogged hill-scene on an enormous continent,
intimacy rigged with terrors,
a sequence of blurs the Chinese painter's ink-stick planned,

a scene of desolation comforted
by two human figures recklessly exposed,
leaning together in a sticklike boat
in the foreground. Maybe we look like this,
I don't know. I'm wondering
whether we even have what we think we have—
lighted windows signifying shelter,
a film of domesticity
over fragile roofs. I know I'm partly somewhere else—
huts strung across a drought-stretched land
not mine, dried breasts, mine and not mine, a mother
watching my children shrink with hunger.
I live in my Western skin,
my Western vision, torn
and flung to what I can't control or even fathom.
Quantify suffering, you could rule the world.

2.

They cán rule the world while they can persuade us
our pain belongs in some order.
Is death by famine worse than death by suicide,
than a life of famine and suicide, if a black lesbian dies,
if a white prostitute dies, if a woman genius
starves herself to feed others,
self-hatred battening on her body?
Something that kills us or leaves us half-alive
is raging under the name of an "act of god"
in Chad, in Niger, in the Upper Volta—
yes, that male god that acts on us and on our children,
that male State that acts on us and on our children
till our brains are blunted by malnutrition,
yet sharpened by the passion for survival,
our powers expended daily on the struggle
to hand a kind of life on to our children,
to change reality for our lovers
even in a single trembling drop of water.

3.

We can look at each other through both our lifetimes
like those two figures in the sticklike boat
flung together in the Chinese ink-scene;
even our intimacies are rigged with terror.
Quantify suffering? My guilt at least is open,
I stand convicted by all my convictions—
you, too. We shrink from touching
our power, we shrink away, we starve ourselves
and each other, we're scared shitless
of what it could be to take and use our love,
hose it on a city, on a world,
to wield and guide its spray, destroying
poisons, parasites, rats, viruses—
like the terrible mothers we long and dread to be.

4.

The decision to feed the world
is the real decision. No revolution
has chosen it. For that choice requires
that women shall be free.
I choke on the taste of bread in North America
but the taste of hunger in North America
is poisoning me. Yes, I'm alive to write these words,
to leaf through Kollwitz's women
huddling the stricken children into their stricken arms
the "mothers" drained of milk, the "survivors" driven
to self-abortion, self-starvation, to a vision
bitter, concrete, and wordless.
I'm alive to want more than life,
want it for others starving and unborn,
to name the deprivations boring
into my will, my affections, into the brains
of daughters, sisters, lovers caught in the crossfire
of terrorists of the mind.
In the black mirror of the subway window
hangs my own face, hollow with anger and desire.

Swathed in exhaustion, on the trampled newsprint,
a woman shields a dead child from the camera.
The passion to be inscribes her body.
Until we find each other, we are alone.

1974–1975

Cartographies of Silence

1.

A conversation begins
with a lie. And each

speaker of the so-called common language feels
the ice-floe split, the drift apart

as if powerless, as if up against
a force of nature

A poem can begin
with a lie. And be torn up.

A conversation has other laws
recharges itself with its own

false energy. Cannot be torn
up. Infiltrates our blood. Repeats itself.

Inscribes with its unreturning stylus
the isolation it denies.

2.

The classical music station
playing hour upon hour in the apartment

●

the picking up and picking up
and again picking up the telephone

The syllables uttering
the old script over and over

The loneliness of the liar
living in the formal network of the lie

twisting the dials to drown the terror
beneath the unsaid word

3.

The technology of silence
The rituals, etiquette

the blurring of terms
silence not absence

of words or music or even
raw sounds

Silence can be a plan
rigorously executed

the blueprint to a life

It is a presence
it has a history   a form

Do not confuse it
with any kind of absence

4.

How calm, how inoffensive these words
begin to seem to me

though begun in grief and anger
Can I break through this film of the abstract

without wounding myself or you
there is enough pain here

This is why the classical or the jazz music station plays?
to give a ground of meaning to our pain?

5.

The silence that strips bare:
In Dreyer's *Passion of Joan*

Falconetti's face, hair shorn, a great geography
mutely surveyed by the camera

If there were a poetry where this could happen
not as blank spaces or as words

stretched like a skin over meanings
but as silence falls at the end

of a night through which two people
have talked till dawn

6.

The scream
of an illegitimate voice

It has ceased to hear itself, therefore
it asks itself

How dó I exist?

This was the silence I wanted to break in you
I had questions but you would not answer

•

I had answers but you could not use them
This is useless to you and perhaps to others

7.

It was an old theme even for me:
Language cannot do everything—

chalk it on the walls where the dead poets
lie in their mausoleums

If at the will of the poet the poem
could turn into a thing

a granite flank laid bare, a lifted head
alight with dew

If it could simply look you in the face
with naked eyeballs, not letting you turn

till you, and I who long to make this thing,
were finally clarified together in its stare

8.

No. Let me have this dust,
these pale clouds dourly lingering, these words

moving with ferocious accuracy
like the blind child's fingers

or the newborn infant's mouth
violent with hunger

No one can give me, I have long ago
taken this method

whether of bran pouring from the loose-woven sack
or of the bunsen-flame turned low and blue

•

If from time to time I envy
the pure annunciations to the eye

the *visio beatifica*
if from time to time I long to turn

like the Eleusinian hierophant
holding up a simple ear of grain

for return to the concrete and everlasting world
what in fact I keep choosing

are these words, these whispers, conversations
from which time after time the truth breaks moist and green.

1975

Twenty-One Love Poems

I

Wherever in this city, screens flicker
with pornography, with science-fiction vampires,
victimized hirelings bending to the lash,
we also have to walk . . . if simply as we walk
through the rainsoaked garbage, the tabloid cruelties
of our own neighborhoods.
We need to grasp our lives inseparable
from those rancid dreams, that blurt of metal, those disgraces,
and the red begonia perilously flashing
from a tenement sill six stories high,
or the long-legged young girls playing ball
in the junior highschool playground.
No one has imagined us. We want to live like trees,
sycamores blazing through the sulfuric air,
dappled with scars, still exuberantly budding,
our animal passion rooted in the city.

●

II

I wake up in your bed. I know I have been dreaming.
Much earlier, the alarm broke us from each other,
you've been at your desk for hours. I know what I dreamed:
our friend the poet comes into my room
where I've been writing for days,
drafts, carbons, poems are scattered everywhere,
and I want to show her one poem
which is the poem of my life. But I hesitate,
and wake. You've kissed my hair
to wake me. *I dreamed you were a poem,*
I say, *a poem I wanted to show someone . . .*
and I laugh and fall dreaming again
of the desire to show you to everyone I love,
to move openly together
in the pull of gravity, which is not simple,
which carries the feathered grass a long way down the upbreathing air.

III

Since we're not young, weeks have to do time
for years of missing each other. Yet only this odd warp
in time tells me we're not young.
Did I ever walk the morning streets at twenty,
my limbs streaming with a purer joy?
did I lean from any window over the city
listening for the future
as I listen here with nerves tuned for your ring?
And you, you move toward me with the same tempo.
Your eyes are everlasting, the green spark
of the blue-eyed grass of early summer,
the green-blue wild cress washed by the spring.
At twenty, yes: we thought we'd live forever.
At forty-five, I want to know even our limits.
I touch you knowing we weren't born tomorrow,
and somehow, each of us will help the other live,
and somewhere, each of us must help the other die.

•

IV

I come home from you through the early light of spring
flashing off ordinary walls, the Pez Dorado,
the Discount Wares, the shoe-store. . . . I'm lugging my sack
of groceries, I dash for the elevator
where a man, taut, elderly, carefully composed
lets the door almost close on me. —*For god's sake hold it!*
I croak at him. —*Hysterical,*—he breathes my way.
I let myself into the kitchen, unload my bundles,
make coffee, open the window, put on Nina Simone
singing *Here comes the sun.* . . . I open the mail,
drinking delicious coffee, delicious music,
my body still both light and heavy with you. The mail
lets fall a Xerox of something written by a man
aged 27, a hostage, tortured in prison:
*My genitals have been the object of such a sadistic display
they keep me constantly awake with the pain . . .*
Do whatever you can to survive.
You know, I think that men love wars . . .
And my incurable anger, my unmendable wounds
break open further with tears, I am crying helplessly,
and they still control the world, and you are not in my arms.

V

This apartment full of books could crack open
to the thick jaws, the bulging eyes
of monsters, easily: Once open the books, you have to face
the underside of everything you've loved—
the rack and pincers held in readiness, the gag
even the best voices have had to mumble through,
the silence burying unwanted children—
women, deviants, witnesses—in desert sand.
Kenneth tells me he's been arranging his books
so he can look at Blake and Kafka while he types;
yes; and we still have to reckon with Swift
loathing the woman's flesh while praising her mind,
Goethe's dread of the Mothers, Claudel vilifying Gide,

and the ghosts—their hands clasped for centuries—
of artists dying in childbirth, wise-women charred at the stake,
centuries of books unwritten piled behind these shelves;
and we still have to stare into the absence
of men who would not, women who could not, speak
to our life—this still unexcavated hole
called civilization, this act of translation, this half-world.

VI

Your small hands, precisely equal to my own—
only the thumb is larger, longer—in these hands
I could trust the world, or in many hands like these,
handling power-tools or steering-wheel
or touching a human face. . . . Such hands could turn
the unborn child rightways in the birth canal
or pilot the exploratory rescue-ship
through icebergs, or piece together
the fine, needle-like sherds of a great krater-cup
bearing on its sides
figures of esctatic women striding
to the sibyl's den or the Eleusinian cave—
such hands might carry out an unavoidable violence
with such restraint, with such a grasp
of the range and limits of violence
that violence ever after would be obsolete.

VII

What kind of beast would turn its life into words?
What atonement is this all about?
—and yet, writing words like these, I'm also living.
Is all this close to the wolverines' howled signals,
that modulated cantata of the wild?
or, when away from you I try to create you in words,
am I simply using you, like a river or a war?
And how have I used rivers, how have I used wars
to escape writing of the worst thing of all—
not the crimes of others, not even our own death,

but the failure to want our freedom passionately enough
so that blighted elms, sick rivers, massacres would seem
mere emblems of that desecration of ourselves?

VIII

I can see myself years back at Sunion,
hurting with an infected foot, Philoctetes
in woman's form, limping the long path,
lying on a headland over the dark sea,
looking down the red rocks to where a soundless curl
of white told me a wave had struck,
imagining the pull of that water from that height,
knowing deliberate suicide wasn't my métier,
yet all the time nursing, measuring that wound.
Well, that's finished. The woman who cherished
her suffering is dead. I am her descendant.
I love the scar-tissue she handed on to me,
but I want to go on from here with you
fighting the temptation to make a career of pain.

IX

Your silence today is a pond where drowned things live
I want to see raised dripping and brought into the sun.
It's not my own face I see there, but other faces,
even your face at another age.
Whatever's lost there is needed by both of us—
a watch of old gold, a water-blurred fever chart,
a key. . . . Even the silt and pebbles of the bottom
deserve their glint of recognition. I fear this silence,
this inarticulate life. I'm waiting
for a wind that will gently open this sheeted water
for once, and show me what I can do
for you, who have often made the unnameable
nameable for others, even for me.

•

X

Your dog, tranquil and innocent, dozes through
our cries, our murmured dawn conspiracies
our telephone calls. She knows—what can she know?
If in my human arrogance I claim to read
her eyes, I find there only my own animal thoughts:
that creatures must find each other for bodily comfort,
that voices of the psyche drive through the flesh
further than the dense brain could have foretold,
that the planetary nights are growing cold for those
on the same journey, who want to touch
one creature-traveler clear to the end;
that without tenderness, we are in hell.

XI

Every peak is a crater. This is the law of volcanoes,
making them eternally and visibly female.
No height without depth, without a burning core,
though our straw soles shred on the hardened lava.
I want to travel with you to every sacred mountain
smoking within like the sibyl stooped over his tripod,
I want to reach for your hand as we scale the path,
to feel your arteries glowing in my clasp,
never failing to note the small, jewel-like flower
unfamiliar to us, nameless till we rename her,
that clings to the slowly altering rock—
that detail outside ourselves that brings us to ourselves,
was here before us, knew we would come, and sees beyond us.

XII

Sleeping, turning in turn like planets
rotating in their midnight meadow:
a touch is enough to let us know
we're not alone in the universe, even in sleep:
the dream-ghosts of two worlds
walking their ghost-towns, almost address each other.
I've wakened to your muttered words

spoken light- or dark-years away
as if my own voice had spoken.
But we have different voices, even in sleep,
and our bodies, so alike, are yet so different
and the past echoing through our bloodstreams
is freighted with different language, different meanings—
though in any chronicle of the world we share
it could be written with new meaning
we were two lovers of one gender,
we were two women of one generation.

XIII

The rules break like a thermometer,
quicksilver spills across the charted systems,
we're out in a country that has no language
no laws, we're chasing the raven and the wren
through gorges unexplored since dawn
whatever we do together is pure invention
the maps they gave us were out of date
by years . . . we're driving through the desert
wondering if the water will hold out
the hallucinations turn to simple villages
the music on the radio comes clear—
neither *Rosenkavalier* nor *Götterdämmerung*
but a woman's voice singing old songs
with new words, with a quiet bass, a flute
plucked and fingered by women outside the law.

XIV

It was your vision of the pilot
confirmed my vision of you: you said, *He keeps
on steering headlong into the waves, on purpose*
while we crouched in the open hatchway
vomiting into plastic bags
for three hours between St. Pierre and Miquelon.
I never felt closer to you.
In the close cabin where the honeymoon couples

huddled in each other's laps and arms
I put my hand on your thigh
to comfort both of us, your hand came over mine,
we stayed that way, suffering together
in our bodies, as if all suffering
were physical, we touched so in the presence
of strangers who knew nothing and cared less
vomiting their private pain
as if all suffering were physical.

(THE FLOATING POEM, UNNUMBERED)

Whatever happens with us, your body
will haunt mine—tender, delicate
your lovemaking, like the half-curled frond
of the fiddlehead fern in forests
just washed by sun. Your traveled, generous thighs
between which my whole face has come and come—
the innocence and wisdom of the place my tongue has found there—
the live, insatiate dance of your nipples in my mouth—
your touch on me, firm, protective, searching
me out, your strong tongue and slender fingers
reaching where I had been waiting years for you
in my rose-wet cave—whatever happens, this is.

XV

If I lay on that beach with you
white, empty, pure green water warmed by the Gulf Stream
and lying on that beach we could not stay
because the wind drove fine sand against us
as if it were against us
if we tried to withstand it and we failed—
if we drove to another place
to sleep in each other's arms
and the beds were narrow like prisoners' cots
and we were tired and did not sleep together
and this was what we found, so this is what we did—
was the failure ours?

If I cling to circumstances I could feel
not responsible. Only she who says
she did not choose, is the loser in the end.

XVI

Across a city from you, I'm with you,
just as an August night
moony, inlet-warm, seabathed, I watched you sleep,
the scrubbed, sheenless wood of the dressing-table
cluttered with our brushes, books, vials in the moonlight—
or a salt-mist orchard, lying at your side
watching red sunset through the screendoor of the cabin,
G minor Mozart on the tape-recorder,
falling asleep to the music of the sea.
This island of Manhattan is wide enough
for both of us, and narrow:
I can hear your breath tonight, I know how your face
lies upturned, the halflight tracing
your generous, delicate mouth
where grief and laughter sleep together.

XVII

No one's fated or doomed to love anyone.
The accidents happen, we're not heroines,
they happen in our lives like car crashes,
books that change us, neighborhoods
we move into and come to love.
Tristan und Isolde is scarcely the story,
women at least should know the difference
between love and death. No poison cup,
no penance. Merely a notion that the tape-recorder
should have caught some ghost of us: that tape-recorder
not merely played but should have listened to us,
and could instruct those after us:
this we were, this is how we tried to love,
and these are the forces they had ranged against us,
and these are the forces we had ranged within us,
within us and against us, against us and within us.

•

XVIII

Rain on the West Side Highway,
red light at Riverside:
the more I live the more I think
two people together is a miracle.
You're telling the story of your life
for once, a tremor breaks the surface of your words.
The story of our lives becomes our lives.
Now you're in fugue across what some I'm sure
Victorian poet called the *salt estranging sea.*
Those are the words that come to mind.
I feel estrangement, yes. As I've felt dawn
pushing toward daybreak. Something: a cleft of light—?
Close between grief and anger, a space opens
where I am Adrienne alone. And growing colder.

XIX

Can it be growing colder when I begin
to touch myself again, adhesions pull away?
When slowly the naked face turns from staring backward
and looks into the present,
the eye of winter, city, anger, poverty, and death
and the lips part and say: *I mean to go on living?*
Am I speaking coldly when I tell you in a dream
or in this poem, *There are no miracles?*
(I told you from the first I wanted daily life,
this island of Manhattan was island enough for me.)
If I could let you know—
two women together is a work
nothing in civilization has made simple,
two people together is a work
heroic in its ordinariness,
the slow-picked, halting traverse of a pitch
where the fiercest attention becomes routine
—look at the faces of those who have chosen it.

•

XX

That conversation we were always on the edge
of having, runs on in my head,
at night the Hudson trembles in New Jersey light
polluted water yet reflecting even
sometimes the moon
and I discern a woman
I loved, drowning in secrets, fear wound round her throat
and choking her like hair. And this is she
with whom I tried to speak, whose hurt, expressive head
turning aside from pain, is dragged down deeper
where it cannot hear me,
and soon I shall know I was talking to my own soul.

XXI

The dark lintels, the blue and foreign stones
of the great round rippled by stone implements
the midsummer night light rising from beneath
the horizon—when I said "a cleft of light"
I meant this. And this is not Stonehenge
simply nor any place but the mind
casting back to where her solitude,
shared, could be chosen without loneliness,
not easily nor without pains to stake out
the circle, the heavy shadows, the great light.
I choose to be a figure in that light,
half-blotted by darkness, something moving
across that space, the color of stone
greeting the moon, yet more than stone:
a woman. I choose to walk here. And to draw this circle.

1974–1976

Upper Broadway

The leafbud straggles forth
toward the frigid light of the airshaft   this is faith
this pale extension of a day
when looking up   you know   something is changing
winter has turned   though the wind is colder
Three streets away   a roof collapses   onto people
who thought they still had time   Time out of mind

I have written so many words
wanting to live inside you
to be of use to you

Now I must write for myself   for this blind
woman scratching the pavement   with her wand of thought
this slippered crone   inching on icy streets
reaching into wire trashbaskets   pulling out
what was thrown away   and infinitely precious

I look at hands and see   they are still unfinished
I look at the vine and see the leafbud
inching towards life

I look at my face in the glass   and see
a halfborn woman

1975

Paula Becker to Clara Westhoff

Paula Becker 1876–1907
Clara Westhoff 1878–1954

became friends at Worpswede, an artists' colony near
Bremen, Germany, summer 1899. In January 1900, spent
a half-year together in Paris, where Paula painted and Clara
studied sculpture with Rodin. In August they returned to
Worpswede, and spent the next winter together in Berlin.
In 1901, Clara married the poet Rainer Maria Rilke; soon
after, Paula married the painter Otto Modersohn. She died
in a hemorrhage after childbirth, murmuring, *What a shame!*

The autumn feels slowed down,
summer still holds on here, even the light
seems to last longer than it should
or maybe I'm using it to the thin edge.
The moon rolls in the air. I didn't want this child.
You're the only one I've told.
I want a child maybe, someday, but not now.
Otto has a calm, complacent way
of following me with his eyes, as if to say
Soon you'll have your hands full!
And yes, I will; this child will be mine
not his, the failures, if I fail
will be all mine. We're not good, Clara,
at learning to prevent these things,
and once we have a child, it *is* ours.
But lately, I feel beyond Otto or anyone.
I know now the kind of work I have to do.
It takes such energy! I have the feeling I'm
moving somewhere, patiently, impatiently,
in my loneliness. I'm looking everywhere in nature
for new forms, old forms in new places,
the planes of an antique mouth, let's say, among the leaves.
I know and do not know

what I am searching for.
Remember those months in the studio together,
you up to your strong forearms in wet clay,
I trying to make something of the strange impressions
assailing me—the Japanese
flowers and birds on silk, the drunks
sheltering in the Louvre, that river-light,
those faces. . . . Did we know exactly
why we were there? Paris unnerved you,
you found it too much, yet you went on
with your work . . . and later we met there again,
both married then, and I thought you and Rilke
both seemed unnerved. I felt a kind of joylessness
between you. Of course he and I
have had our difficulties. Maybe I was jealous
of him, to begin with, taking you from me,
maybe I married Otto to fill up
my loneliness for you.
Rainer, of course, *knows* more than Otto knows,
he believes in women. But he feeds on us,
like all of them. His whole life, his art
is protected by women. Which of us could say that?
Which of us, Clara, hasn't had to take that leap
out beyond our being women
to save our work? or is it to save ourselves?
Marriage is lonelier that solitude.
Do you know: I was dreaming I had died
giving birth to the child.
I couldn't paint or speak or even move.
My child—I think—survived me. But what was funny
in the dream was, Rainer had written my requiem—
a long, beautiful poem, and calling me his friend.
I was *your* friend
but in the dream you didn't say a word.
In the dream his poem was like a letter
to someone who has no right
to be there but must be treated gently, like a guest
who comes on the wrong day. Clara, why don't I dream of you?

That photo of the two of us—I have it still,
you and I looking hard into each other
and my painting behind us. How we used to work
side by side! And how I've worked since then
trying to create according to our plan
that we'd bring, against all odds, our full power
to every subject. Hold back nothing
because we were women. Clara, our strength still lies
in the things we used to talk about:
how life and death take one another's hands,
the struggle for truth, our old pledge against guilt.
And now I feel dawn and the coming day.
I love waking in my studio, seeing my pictures
come alive in the light. Sometimes I feel
it is myself that kicks inside me,
myself I must give suck to, love . . .
I wish we could have done this for each other
all our lives, but we can't . . .
They say a pregnant woman
dreams of her own death. But life and death
take one another's hands. Clara, I feel so full
of work, the life I see ahead, and love
for you, who of all people
however badly I say this
will hear all I say and cannot say.

1975–1976

A Woman Dead in Her Forties

1.

Your breasts/   sliced-off   The scars
dimmed   as they would have to be
years later

•

All the women I grew up with are sitting
half-naked on rocks   in sun
we look at each other and
are not ashamed

and you too have taken off your blouse
but this was not what you wanted:

to show your scarred, deleted torso

I barely glance at you
as if my look could scald you
though I'm the one who loved you

I want to touch my fingers
to where your breasts had been
but we never did such things

You hadn't thought everyone
would look so perfect
unmutilated

you pull on
your blouse again: stern statement:

*There are things I will not share
with everyone*

2.

You send me back to share
My own scars   first of all
with myself

What did I hide from her
what have I denied her
what losses suffered

how in this ignorant body
did she hide

waiting for her release
till uncontrollable light began to pour

from every wound and suture
and all the sacred openings

3.

Wartime.   We sit on warm
weathered, softening grey boards

the ladder glimmers where you told me
the leeches swim

I smell the flame
of kerosene   the pine

boards where we sleep side by side
in narrow cots

the night-meadow exhaling
its darkness   calling

child into woman
child into woman
woman

4.

Most of our love from the age of nine
took the form of jokes and mute

loyalty: you fought a girl
who said she'd knock me down

we did each other's homework
wrote letters   kept in touch, untouching

•

lied about our lives: I wearing
the face of the proper marriage

you the face of the independent woman
We cleaved to each other across that space

fingering webs
of love and estrangement   till the day

the gynecologist touched your breast
and found a palpable hardness

5.

You played heroic, necessary
games with death

since in your neo-protestant tribe the void
was supposed not to exist

except as a fashionable concept
you had no traffic with

I wish you were here tonight   I want
to yell at you

Don't accept
Don't give in

But would I be meaning your brave
irreproachable life, you dean of women, or

your unfair, unfashionable, unforgivable
woman's death?

6.

You are every woman I ever loved
and disavowed

a bloody incandescent chord strung out
across years, tracts of space

How can I reconcile this passion
with our modesty

your calvinist heritage
my girlhood frozen into forms

how can I go on this mission
without you

you, who might have told me
everything you feel is true?

7.

Time after time in dreams you rise
reproachful

once from a wheelchair pushed by your father
across a lethal expressway

Of all my dead it's you
who come to me unfinished

You left me amber beads
strung with turquoise from an Egyptian grave

I wear them wondering
How am I true to you?

I'm half-afraid to write poetry
for you   who never read it much

and I'm left laboring
with the secrets and the silence

•

in plain language: I never told you how I loved you
we never talked at your deathbed of your death

8.

One autumn evening in a train
catching the diamond-flash of sunset

in puddles along the Hudson
I thought: *I understand*

life and death now, the choices
I didn't know your choice

or how by then you had no choice
how the body tells the truth in its rush of cells

Most of our love took the form
of mute loyalty

we never spoke at your deathbed of your death

but from here on
I want more crazy mourning, more howl, more keening

We stayed mute and disloyal
because we were afraid

I would have touched my fingers
to where your breasts had been
but we never did such things

1974–1977

Mother-Right

—for M. H.

Woman and child   running
in a field   A man planted
on the horizon

Two hands   one long, slim   one
small, starlike   clasped
in the razor wind

Her hair cut short for faster travel
the child's curls grazing his shoulders
the hawk-winged cloud   over their heads

The man is walking boundaries
measuring   He believes in what is his
the grass   the waters underneath   the air

the air   through which child and mother
are running   the boy singing
the woman   eyes sharpened in the light
heart stumbling   making for the open

1977

Natural Resources

1.

The core of the strong hill: not understood:
the mulch-heat of the underwood

●

where unforeseen the forest fire unfurls;
the heat, the privacy of the mines;

the rainbow laboring to extend herself
where neither men nor cattle understand,

arching her lusters over rut and stubble
purely to reach where she must go;

the emerald lying against the silver vein
waiting for light to reach it, breathing in pain;

the miner laboring beneath
the ray of the headlamp: a weight like death.

2.

The miner is no metaphor. She goes
into the cage like the rest, is flung

downward by gravity like them, must change
her body like the rest to fit a crevice

to work a lode
on her the pick hangs heavy, the bad air

lies thick, the mountain presses in on her
with boulder, timber, fog

slowly the mountain's dust descends
into the fibers of her lungs.

3.

The cage drops into the dark,
the routine of life goes on:

a woman turns a doorknob, but so slowly
so quietly, that no one wakes

●

and it is she alone who gazes
into the dark of bedrooms, ascertains

how they sleep, who needs her touch
what window blows the ice of February

into the room and who must be protected:
It is only she who sees; who was trained to see.

4.

Could you imagine a world of women only,
the interviewer asked. *Can you imagine*

a world where women are absent. (He believed
he was joking.) Yet I have to imagine

at one and the same moment, both. Because
I live in both. *Can you imagine,*

the interviewer asked, *a world of men?*
(He thought he was joking.) *If so, then,*

a world where men are absent?
Absently, wearily, I answered: Yes.

5.

The phantom of the man-who-would-understand,
the lost brother, the twin—

for him did we leave our mothers,
deny our sisters, over and over?

did we invent him, conjure him
over the charring log,

nights, late, in the snowbound cabin
did we dream or scry his face

•

in the liquid embers,
the man-who-would-dare-to-know-us?

6.

It was never the rapist:
it was the brother, lost,

the comrade/twin whose palm
would bear a lifeline like our own:

decisive, arrowy,
forked-lightning of insatiate desire

It was never the crude pestle, the blind
ramrod we were after:

merely a fellow-creature
with natural resources equal to our own

7.

Meanwhile, another kind of being
was constructing itself, blindly

—a mutant, some have said:
the blood-compelled exemplar

of a "botched civilization"
as one of them called it

children picking up guns
for that is what it means to be a man

We have lived with violence for seven years
It was not worth one single life—

but the patriot's fist is at her throat,
her voice is in mortal danger

•

and that kind of being has lain in our beds
declaring itself our desire

requiring women's blood for life
a woman's breast to lay its nightmare on

8.

And that kind of being has other forms:
a passivity we mistake

—in the desperation of our search—
for gentleness

But gentleness is active
gentleness swabs the crusted stump

invents more merciful instruments
to touch the wound beyond the wound

does not faint with disgust
will not be driven off

keeps bearing witness calmly
against the predator, the parasite

9.

I am tired of faintheartedness,
their having to be *exceptional*

to do what an ordinary woman
does in the course of things

I am tired of women stooping to half our height
to bring the essential vein to light

tired of the waste of what we bear
with such cost, such elation, into sight

•

(—for what becomes of what the miner probes
and carves from the mountain's body in her pain?)

10.

This is what I am: watching the spider
rebuild—"patiently", they say,

but I recognize in her
impatience—my own—

the passion to make and make again
where such unmaking reigns

the refusal to be a victim
we have lived with violence so long

Am I to go on saying
for myself, for her

This is my body,
take and destroy it?

11.

The enormity of the simplest things:
in this cold barn tables are spread

with china saucers, shoehorns
of german silver, a gilt-edged book

that opens into picture-frame—
a biscuit-tin of the thirties.

Outside, the north lies vast
with unshed snow, everything is

at once remote and familiar
each house contains what it must

•

women simmer carcasses
of clean-picked turkeys, store away

the cleaned cutglass and soak the linen cloths
Dark rushes early at the panes

12.

These things by women saved
are all we have of them

or of those dear to them
these ribboned letters, snapshots

faithfully glued for years
onto the scrapbook page

these scraps, turned into patchwork,
doll-gowns, clean white rags

for stanching blood
the bride's tea-yellow handkerchief

the child's height penciled on the cellar door
In this cold barn we dream

a universe of humble things—
and without these, no memory

no faithfulness, no purpose for the future
no honor to the past

13.

There are words I cannot choose again:
humanism   androgyny

Such words have no shame in them, no diffidence
before the raging stoic grandmothers:

•

their glint is too shallow, like a dye
that does not permeate

the fibers of actual life
as we live it, now:

this fraying blanket with its ancient stains
we pull across the sick child's shoulder

or wrap around the senseless legs
of the hero trained to kill

this weaving, ragged because incomplete
we turn our hands to, interrupted

over and over, handed down
unfinished, found in the drawer

of an old dresser in the barn,
her vanished pride and care

still urging us, urging on
our works, to close the gap

in the Great Nebula,
to help the earth deliver.

14.

The women who first knew themselves
miners, are dead. The rainbow flies

like a flying buttress from the walls
of cloud, the silver-and-green vein

awaits the battering of the pick
the dark lode weeps for light

●

My heart is moved by all I cannot save:
so much has been destroyed

I have to cast my lot with those
who age after age, perversely,

with no extraordinary power,
reconstitute the world.

1977

Transcendental Etude

—for Michelle Cliff

This August evening I've been driving
over backroads fringed with queen anne's lace
my car startling young deer in meadows—one
gave a hoarse intake of her breath and all
four fawns sprang after her
into the dark maples.
Three months from today they'll be fair game
for the hit-and-run hunters, glorying
in a weekend's destructive power,
triggers fingered by drunken gunmen, sometimes
so inept as to leave the shattered animal
stunned in her blood. But this evening deep in summer
the deer are still alive and free,
nibbling apples from early-laden boughs
so weighted, so englobed
with already yellowing fruit
they seem eternal, Hesperidean
in the clear-tuned, cricket-throbbing air.

Later I stood in the dooryard,
my nerves singing the immense

fragility of all this sweetness,
this green world already sentimentalized, photographed,
advertised to death. Yet, it persists
stubbornly beyond the fake Vermont
of antique barnboards glazed into discothèques,
artificial snow, the sick Vermont of children
conceived in apathy, grown to winters
of rotgut violence,
poverty gnashing its teeth like a blind cat at their lives.
Still, it persists. Turning off onto a dirt road
from the raw cuts bulldozed through a quiet village
for the tourist run to Canada,
I've sat on a stone fence above a great, soft, sloping field
of musing heifers, a farmstead
slanting its planes calmly in the calm light,
a dead elm raising bleached arms
above a green so dense with life,
minute, momentary life—slugs, moles, pheasants, gnats,
spiders, moths, hummingbirds, groundhogs, butterflies—
a lifetime is too narrow
to understand it all, beginning with the huge
rockshelves that underlie all that life.

No one ever told us we had to study our lives,
make of our lives a study, as if learning natural history
or music, that we should begin
with the simple exercises first
and slowly go on trying
the hard ones, practicing till strength
and accuracy became one with the daring
to leap into transcendence, take the chance
of breaking down in the wild arpeggio
or faulting the full sentence of the fugue.
—And in fact we can't live like that: we take on
everything at once before we've even begun
to read or mark time, we're forced to begin
in the midst of the hardest movement,
the one already sounding as we are born.

At most we're allowed a few months
of simply listening to the simple line
of a woman's voice singing a child
against her heart. Everything else is too soon,
too sudden, the wrenching-apart, that woman's heartbeat
heard ever after from a distance,
the loss of that ground-note echoing
whenever we are happy, or in despair.

Everything else seems beyond us,
we aren't ready for it, nothing that was said
is true for us, caught naked in the argument,
the counterpoint, trying to sightread
what our fingers can't keep up with, learn by heart
what we can't even read. And yet
it *is* this we were born to. We aren't virtuosi
or child prodigies, there are no prodigies
in this realm, only a half-blind, stubborn
cleaving to the timbre, the tones of what we are
—even when all the texts describe it differently.

And we're not performers, like Liszt, competing
against the world for speed and brilliance
(the 79-year-old pianist said, when I asked her
What makes a virtuoso?—Competitiveness.)
The longer I live the more I mistrust
theatricality, the false glamour cast
by performance, the more I know its poverty beside
the truths we are salvaging from
the splitting-open of our lives.
The woman who sits watching, listening,
eyes moving in the darkness
is rehearsing in her body, hearing-out in her blood
a score touched off in her perhaps
by some words, a few chords, from the stage:
a tale only she can tell.

But there come times—perhaps this is one of them—
when we have to take ourselves more seriously or die;

when we have to pull back from the incantations,
rhythms we've moved to thoughtlessly,
and disenthrall ourselves, bestow
ourselves to silence, or a severer listening, cleansed
of oratory, formulas, choruses, laments, static
crowding the wires. We cut the wires,
find ourselves in free-fall, as if
our true home were the undimensional
solitudes, the rift
in the Great Nebula.
No one who survives to speak
new language, has avoided this:
the cutting-away of an old force that held her
rooted to an old ground
the pitch of utter loneliness
where she herself and all creation
seem equally dispersed, weightless, her being a cry
to which no echo comes or can ever come.

But in fact we were always like this,
rootless, dismembered: knowing it makes the difference.
Birth stripped our birthright from us,
tore us from a woman, from women, from ourselves
so early on
and the whole chorus throbbing at our ears
like midges, told us nothing, nothing
of origins, nothing we needed
to know, nothing that could re-member us.

Only: that it is unnatural,
the homesickness for a woman, for ourselves,
for that acute joy at the shadow her head and arms
cast on a wall, her heavy or slender
thighs on which we lay, flesh against flesh,
eyes steady on the face of love; smell of her milk, her sweat,
terror of her disappearance, all fused in this hunger
for the element they have called most dangerous, to be
lifted breathtaken on her breast, to rock within her
—even if beaten back, stranded against, to apprehend

in a sudden brine-clear thought
trembling like the tiny, orbed, endangered
egg-sac of a new world:
This is what she was to me, and this
is how I can love myself—
as only a woman can love me.

Homesick for myself, for her—as, after the heatwave
breaks, the clear tones of the world
manifest: cloud, bough, wall, insect, the very soul of light:
homesick as the fluted vault of desire
articulates itself: *I am the lover and the loved,*
home and wanderer, she who splits
firewood and she who knocks, a stranger
in the storm, two women, eye to eye
measuring each other's spirit, each other's
limitless desire,
                    a whole new poetry beginning here.

Vision begins to happen in such a life
as if a woman quietly walked away
from the argument and jargon in a room
and sitting down in the kitchen, began turning in her lap
bits of yarn, calico and velvet scraps,
laying them out absently on the scrubbed boards
in the lamplight, with small rainbow-colored shells
sent in cotton-wool from somewhere far away,
and skeins of milkweed from the nearest meadow—
original domestic silk, the finest findings—
and the darkblue petal of the petunia,
and the dry darkbrown lace of seaweed;
not forgotten either, the shed silver
whisker of the cat,
the spiral of paper-wasp-nest curling
beside the finch's yellow feather.
Such a composition has nothing to do with eternity,
the striving for greatness, brilliance—
only with the musing of a mind

one with her body, experienced fingers quietly pushing
dark against bright, silk against roughness,
pulling the tenets of a life together
with no mere will to mastery,
only care for the many-lived, unending
forms in which she finds herself,
becoming now the sherd of broken glass
slicing light in a corner, dangerous
to flesh, now the plentiful, soft leaf
that wrapped round the throbbing finger, soothes the wound;
and now the stone foundation, rockshelf further
forming underneath everything that grows.

1977

From

*A Wild Patience Has
Taken Me This Far*
1981

Integrity

*the quality or state of being complete; unbroken
condition; entirety*
—Webster

A wild patience has taken me this far

as if I had to bring to shore
a boat with a spasmodic outboard motor
old sweaters, nets, spray-mottled books
tossed in the prow
some kind of sun burning my shoulder-blades.
Splashing the oarlocks. Burning through.
Your fore-arms can get scalded, licked with pain
in a sun blotted like unspoken anger
behind a casual mist.

The length of daylight
this far north, in this
forty-ninth year of my life
is critical.

The light is critical: of me, of this
long-dreamed, involuntary landing
on the arm of an inland sea.
The glitter of the shoal
depleting into shadow
I recognize: the stand of pines
violet-black really, green in the old postcard
but really I have nothing but myself
to go by; nothing
stands in the realm of pure necessity
except what my hands can hold.

•

273

Nothing but myself? . . . My selves.
After so long, this answer.
As if I had always known
I steer the boat in, simply.
The motor dying on the pebbles
cicadas taking up the hum
dropped in the silence.

Anger and tenderness: my selves.
And now I can believe they breathe in me
as angels, not polarities.
Anger and tenderness: the spider's genius
to spin and weave in the same action
from her own body, anywhere—
even from a broken web.

The cabin in the stand of pines
is still for sale. I know this. Know the print
of the last foot, the hand that slammed and locked that door,
then stopped to wreathe the rain-smashed clematis
back on the trellis
for no one's sake except its own.
I know the chart nailed to the wallboards
the icy kettle squatting on the burner.
The hands that hammered in those nails
emptied that kettle one last time
are these two hands
and they have caught the baby leaping
from between trembling legs
and they have worked the vacuum aspirator
and stroked the sweated temples
and steered the boat here through this hot
misblotted sunlight, critical light
imperceptibly scalding
the skin these hands will also salve.

1978

Culture and Anarchy

Leafshade stirring on lichened bark
                              Daylilies
run wild, "escaped" the botanists call it
from dooryard to meadow to roadside

Life-tingle of angled light
                         late summer
sharpening toward fall, each year more sharply

This headlong, loved, escaping life

Rainy days at the kitchen table typing,
heaped up letters, a dry moth's
perfectly mosaiced wings, pamphlets on rape,
forced sterilization, snapshots in color
of an Alabama woman still quilting in her nineties,
The Life and Work of Susan B. Anthony. . . .

> *I stained and varnished*
> *the library bookcase today and superintended*
> *the plowing of the orchard.* . . .
> *Fitted out a fugitive slave for Canada*
> *with the help of Harriet Tubman.* . . .
> *The women's committee failed*
> *to report. I am mortified to death for them.* . . .
> *Washed every window in the house today.*
> *Put a quilted petticoat in the frame.*
> *Commenced Mrs. Browning's Portuguese*
> *Sonnets. Have just finished*
> *Casa Guidi Windows, a grand poem*
> *and so fitting to our struggle.* . . .
> *To forever blot out slavery is the only*
> *possible compensation for this*
> *merciless war.* . . .

●

The all-alone feeling will creep over me. . . .

Upstairs, long silence, then
again, the sudden torrent of your typing

Rough drafts we share, each reading
her own page over the other's shoulder
trying to see afresh

An energy I cannot even yet
take for granted: picking up a book
of the nineteenth century, reading there the name
of the woman whose book you found
in the old town Athenaeum
beginning to stitch together
Elizabeth Ellet
Elizabeth Barrett
Elizabeth Blackwell
Frances Kemble
Ida B. Wells-Barnett
Susan B. Anthony

On Saturday Mrs. Ford took us to Haworth,
the home of the Brontë sisters. . . .
A most sad day it was to me
as I looked into the little parlor where
the sisters walked up and down
with their arms around each other
and planned their novels. . . .
How much the world of literature has lost
because of their short and ill-environed lives
we can only guess. . . .

Anarchy of August: as if already
autumnal gases glowed in darkness underground
the meadows roughen, grow guttural
with goldenrod, milkweed's late-summer lilac,
cat-tails, the wild lily brazening,
dooryards overflowing in late, rough-headed

bloom: bushes of orange daisies, purple mallow,
the thistle blazing in her clump of knives,
and the great SUNFLOWER turns

Haze wiping out the hills. Mornings like milk,
the mind wading, treading water, the line of vision blind
the pages of the book cling to the hand
words hang in a suspension
the prism hanging in the windowframe
is blank
A stillness building all day long to thunder
as the weedpod swells and thickens
No one can call this calm

> Jane Addams, marking time
> in Europe: *During most*
> *of that time I was absolutely at sea*
> *so far as any moral purpose was concerned*
> *clinging only to the desire to live*
> *in a really living world*
> *refusing to be content*
> *with a shadowy intellectual*
> *or aesthetic reflection*

finally the bursting of the sky
power, release

by sheets by ropes of water, wind
driving before or after
the book laid face-down on the table
spirit travelling the lines of storm
leaping the torrent   all that water
already smelling of earth

> Elizabeth Barrett to Anna Jameson:
> *. . . and is it possible you think*
> *a woman has no business with questions*
> *like the question of slavery?*
> *Then she had better use a pen no more.*

She had better subside into slavery
and concubinage herself, I think, . . .
and take no rank among thinkers and speakers.

Early dark: still raining; the electricity
out. On the littered table
a transparent globe half-filled
with liquid light, the soaked wick quietly
drinking, turning to flame
that faintly stains the slim glass chimney:
ancient, fragile contrivance

light welling, searching the shadows

Matilda Joslyn Gage; Harriet Tubman;
Ida B. Wells-Barnett; Maria Mitchell;
Anna Howard Shaw; Sojourner Truth;
Elizabeth Cady Stanton; Harriet Hosmer;
Clara Barton; Harriet Beecher Stowe;
Ida Husted Harper; Ernestine Rose

and all those without names
because of their short and ill-environed lives

False dawn. Gossamer tents in wet grass: leaflets
dissolving within hours,
spun of necessity and
leaving no trace

The heavy volumes, calf, with titles in smooth
leather, red and black, gilt letters spelling:
THE HISTORY OF HUMAN SUFFERING

I brush my hand across my eyes
—this is a dream, I think—and read:
THE HISTORY OF WOMAN SUFFRAGE

of a movement
for many years unnoticed

or greatly misrepresented in the public press
its records usually not considered
of sufficient value to be
officially preserved

and conjure up again
THE HISTORY OF HUMAN SUFFERING
like bound back issues of a periodical
stretching for miles
OF HUMAN SUFFERING: borne,
tended, soothed, cauterized,
stanched, cleansed, absorbed, endured
by women

our records usually not considered
of sufficient value to be
officially preserved

The strongest reason
for giving woman all the opportunities
for higher education, for the full
development of her forces of mind and body. . .
the most enlarged freedom of thought and action
a complete emancipation
from all the crippling influences of fear—
is the solitude and personal
responsibility
of her own individual life.

Late afternoon: long silence.
Your notes on yellow foolscap drift on the table
you go down to the garden to pick chard
while the strength is in the leaves
crimson stems veining upward into green
How you have given back to me
my dream of a common language
my solitude of self.
I slice the beetroots to the core,
each one contains a different landscape

of bloodlight filaments, distinct rose-purple
striations like the oldest
strata of a Southwestern canyon
an undiscovered planet laid open in the lens

> *I should miss you more than any other*
> *living being from this earth. . .*
> *Yes, our work is one,*
> *we are one in aim and sympathy*
> *and we should be together. . . .*

1978

For Julia in Nebraska

*Here on the divide between the Republican and the Little Blue lived
some of the most courageous people of the frontier. Their fortunes and
their loves live again in the writings of Willa Cather, daughter of the plains
and interpreter of man's growth in these fields and in the valleys beyond.*

*On this beautiful, ever-changing land, man fought to establish a home.
In her vision of the plow against the sun, symbol of the beauty and im-
portance of work, Willa Cather caught the eternal blending of earth and
sky. . . .*

In the Midwest of Willa Cather
the railroad looks like a braid of hair
a grandmother's strong hands plaited
straight down a grand-daughter's back.
Out there last autumn the streets
dreamed copper-lustre, the fields
of winter wheat whispered long snows yet to fall
we were talking of matrices

and now it's spring again already.
This stormy Sunday lashed with rain
I call you in Nebraska

hear you're planting your garden
sanding and oiling a burl of wood
hear in your voice the intention to
survive the long war between mind and body
and we make a promise to talk
this year, about growing older

and I think: we're making a pledge.
Though not much in books of ritual
is useful between women
we still can make vows together
long distance, in electrical code:
Today you were promising me
to live, and I took your word,
Julia, as if it were my own:
we'll live to grow old and talk about it too.

I've listened to your words
seen you stand by the caldron's glare
rendering grammar by the heat
of your womanly wrath.
Brave linguist, bearing your double axe and shield
painfully honed and polished,
no word lies cool on your tongue
bent on restoring meaning to
our lesbian names, in quiet fury
weaving the chronicle so violently torn.

On this beautiful, ever-changing land
—the historical marker says—
man fought to establish a home
(fought whom? the marker is mute.)
They named this Catherland, for Willa Cather,
lesbian—the marker is mute,
the marker white men set on a soil
of broken treaties, Indian blood,
women wiped out in childbirths, massacres—
for Willa Cather, lesbian,
whose letters were burnt in shame.

•

Dear Julia, Willa knew at her death
that the very air was changing
that her Archbishop's skies
would hardly survive his life
she knew as well that history
is neither your script nor mine
it is the pictograph
from which the young must learn
like Tom Outland, from people
discredited or dead
that it needs a telling as plain
as the prairie, as the tale
of a young girl or an old woman
told by tongues that loved them

And Willa who could not tell
her own story as it was
left us her stern and delicate
respect for the lives she loved—
How are we going to do better?
for that's the question that lies
beyond our excavations,
the question I ask of you
and myself, when our maps diverge,
when we miss signals, fail—

And if I've written in passion,
Live, Julia! what was I writing
but my own pledge to myself
where the love of women is rooted?
And what was I invoking
but the matrices we weave
web upon web, delicate rafters
flung in audacity to the prairie skies
nets of telepathy contrived
to outlast the iron road
laid out in blood across the land they called virgin—
nets, strands, a braid of hair

a grandmother's strong hands plaited
straight down a grand-daughter's back.

1978, 1981

Transit

When I meet the skier she is always
walking, skis and poles shouldered, toward the mountain
free-swinging in worn boots
over the path new-sifted with fresh snow
her greying dark hair almost hidden by
a cap of many colors
her fifty-year-old, strong, impatient body
dressed for cold and speed
her eyes level with mine

And when we pass each other I look into her face
wondering what we have in common
where our minds converge
for we do not pass each other, she passes me
as I halt beside the fence tangled in snow,
she passes me as I shall never pass her
in this life

Yet I remember us together
climbing Chocorua, summer nineteen-forty-five
details of vegetation beyond the timberline
lichens, wildflowers, birds,
amazement when the trail broke out onto the granite ledge
sloped over blue lakes, green pines, giddy air
like dreams of flying

When sisters separate they haunt each other
as she, who I might once have been, haunts me

or is it I who do the haunting
halting and watching on the path
how she appears again through lightly-blowing
crystals, how her strong knees carry her,
how unaware she is, how simple
this is for her, how without let or hindrance
she travels in her body
until the point of passing, where the skier
and the cripple must decide
to recognize each other?

1979

For Memory

Old words: *trust   fidelity*
Nothing new yet to take their place.

I rake leaves, clear the lawn, October grass
painfully green beneath the gold
and in this silent labor thoughts of you
start up
I hear your voice: *disloyalty   betrayal*
stinging the wires

I stuff the old leaves into sacks
and still they fall and still
I see my work undone

One shivering rainswept afternoon
and the whole job to be done over

I can't know what you know
unless you tell me
there are gashes in our understandings
of this world

We came together in a common
fury of direction
barely mentioning difference
(what drew our finest hairs
to fire
the deep, difficult troughs
unvoiced)
I fell through a basement railing
the first day of school and cut my forehead open—
did I ever tell you? More than forty years
and I still remember smelling my own blood
like the smell of a new schoolbook

And did you ever tell me
how your mother called you in from play
and from whom? To what? These atoms filmed by ordinary dust
that common life we each and all bent out of orbit from
to which we must return simply to say
this is where I came from
this is what I knew

The past is not a husk   yet change goes on

Freedom. It isn't once, to walk out
under the Milky Way, feeling the rivers
of light, the fields of dark—
freedom is daily, prose-bound, routine
remembering. Putting together, inch by inch
the starry worlds. From all the lost collections.

1979

For Ethel Rosenberg

*Convicted, with her husband,
of "conspiracy to commit
espionage"; killed in the
electric chair June 19, 1953*

1.

Europe 1953:
throughout my random sleepwalk
the words

scratched on walls, on pavements
painted over railway arches
Liberez les Rosenberg!

Escaping from home I found
home everywhere:
the Jewish question, Communism

marriage itself
a question of loyalty
or punishment

my Jewish father writing me
letters of seventeen pages
finely inscribed harangues

questions of loyalty
and punishment
One week before my wedding

that couple gets the chair
the volts grapple her, don't
kill her fast enough

•

Liberez les Rosenberg!
I hadn't realized
our family arguments were so important

my narrow understanding
of crime   of punishment
no language for this torment

mystery of that marriage
always both faces
on every front page in the world

Something so shocking   so
unfathomable
it must be pushed aside

2.

She sank however into my soul   A weight of sadness
I hardly can register how deep
her memory has sunk   that wife and mother

like so many
who seemed to get nothing out of any of it
except her children

that daughter   of a family
like so many
needing its female monster

she, actually wishing to be   *an artist*
wanting out of poverty
possibly also really wanting
                              revolution

that woman   strapped in the chair
no fear and no regrets
charged by posterity

•

not with selling secrets to the Communists
but with wanting   *to distinguish*
herself   being a bad daughter   a bad mother

And I   walking to my wedding
by the same token a bad daughter   a bad sister
my forces focussed

on that hardly revolutionary effort
Her life and death   the possible
ranges of disloyalty

so painful   so unfathomable
they must be pushed aside
ignored for years

3.

Her mother testifies against her
Her brother testifies against her
After her death

she becomes a natural prey for pornographers
her death itself a scene
her body *sizzling   half-strapped   whipped like a sail*

She becomes the extremest victim
described nonetheless as *rigid of will*
what are her politics by then   no one knows

Her figure sinks into my soul
a drowned statue
sealed in lead

For years it has lain there   unabsorbed
first as part of that dead couple
on the front pages of the world   the week

•

I gave myself in marriage
then slowly severing   drifting apart
a separate death   a life unto itself

no longer *the Rosenbergs*
no longer the chosen scapegoat
the family monster

till I hear how she sang
a prostitute to sleep
in the Women's House of Detention

Ethel Greenglass Rosenberg   would you
have marched to take back the night
collected signatures

for battered women who kill
What would you have to tell us
would you have burst the net

4.

Why do I even want to call her up
to console my pain   (she feels no pain at all)
why do I wish to put such questions

to ease myself   (she feels no pain at all
she   finally burned to death   like so many)
why all this exercise of hindsight?

since   if I imagine her at all
I have to imagine first
the pain inflicted on her   by women

her mother testifies against her
her sister-in-law testifies against her
and how she sees it

•

not the impersonal forces
not the historical reasons
why they might have hated her strength

If I have held her at arm's length till now
if I have still believed it was
my loyalty, my punishment at stake

if I dare imagine her surviving
I must be fair to what she must have lived through
I must allow her to be at last

political in her ways   not in mine
her urgencies perhaps   impervious to mine
defining revolution as she defines it

or, bored to the marrow of her bones
with "politics"
bored with the vast boredom of long pain

small; tiny in fact; in her late sixties
liking her room   her private life
living alone perhaps

no one you could interview
maybe filling a notebook herself
with secrets she has never sold

1980

Mother-in-Law

Tell me something
                         you say
   Not: What are you working on now, is there anyone special,
   how is the job

do you mind coming back to an empty house
what do you do on Sundays
Tell me something . . .
       Some secret
we both know and have never spoken?
Some sentence that could flood with light
your life, mine?
Tell me what daughters tell their mothers
everywhere in the world, and I and only I
even have to ask. . . .
Tell me something.
   Lately, I hear it: Tell me something true,
   daughter-in-law, before we part,
   tell me something true before I die

   And time was when I tried.
You married my son, and so
strange as you are, you're my daughter
Tell me. . . .
   I've been trying to tell you, mother-in-law
   that I think I'm breaking in two
   and half of me doesn't even want to love
   I can polish this table to satin because I don't care
   I am trying to tell you, I envy
   the people in mental hospitals their freedom
   and I can't live on placebos
   or Valium, like you

A cut lemon scours the smell of fish away
You'll feel better when the children are in school
   I would try to tell you, mother-in-law
   but my anger takes fire from yours and in the oven
   the meal bursts into flames
Daughter-in-law, before we part
tell me something true
   I polished the table, mother-in-law
   and scrubbed the knives with half a lemon

the way you showed me to do
I wish I could tell you—
                    Tell me!
They think I'm weak and hold
things back from me. I agreed to this years ago.
Daughter-in-law, strange as you are,
tell me something true

tell me something
                    Your son is dead
ten years, I am a lesbian,
my children are themselves.
Mother-in-law, before we part
shall we try again? Strange as I am,
strange as you are? What do mothers
ask their own daughters, everywhere in the world?
Is there a question?
                    Ask me something.

1980

Heroines

Exceptional
            even deviant
                        you draw your long skirts
across the nineteenth century
                    Your mind
burns long after death
                        not like the harbor beacon
but like a pyre of driftwood
                    on the beach
                            You are spared
illiteracy
            death by pneumonia
                        teeth which leave the gums

the seamstress' clouded eyes
                    the mill-girl's shortening breath
by a collection
            of circumstances
                        soon to be known as
class privilege
            The laws says you can possess nothing
                                in a world
where property is everything
                    You belong first to your father
then to him who
            chooses you
                    if you fail to marry
you are without recourse
                unable to earn
                        a workingman's salary
forbidden to vote
            forbidden to speak
                        in public

if married you are legally dead
                    the law says
you may not bequeath property
                    save to your children
or male kin
        that your husband
                    has the right
of the slaveholder
            to hunt down and re-possess you
                            should you escape
You may inherit slaves
                but have no power to free them
your skin is fair
            you have been taught that light
came
        to the Dark Continent
                    with white power
that the Indians
            live in filth
                    and occult animal rites

Your mother wore corsets
                    to choke her spirit
                                        which if you refuse
you are jeered for refusing
                            you have heard many sermons
and have carried
                your own interpretations
                                        locked in your heart

You are a woman
                strong in health
                                through a collection
of circumstances
                soon to be known
                                as class privilege
which if you break
                the social compact
                                    you lose outright
When you open your mouth in public
                                    human excrement
                                                    is flung at you
you are exceptional
                    in personal circumstance
                                            in indignation
you give up believing
                    in protection
                                in Scripture
in man-made laws
                respectable as you look
                                        you are an outlaw
Your mind burns
                not like the harbor beacon
                                            but like a fire
of fiercer origin
                you begin speaking out
and a great gust of freedom
                            rushes in with your words
yet still you speak
                in the shattered language
                                        of a partial vision

You draw your long skirts
                         deviant
                                   across the nineteenth century
registering injustice
                      failing to make it whole
How can I fail to love
                      your clarity and fury
how can I give you
                  all your due
                               take courage from your courage
honor your exact
                 legacy as it is
recognizing
            as well
                    that it is not enough?

1980

Grandmothers

1. Mary Gravely Jones

We had no petnames, no diminutives for you,
always the formal guest under my father's roof:
you were "Grandmother Jones" and you visited rarely.
I see you walking up and down the garden,
restless, southern-accented, reserved, you did not seem
my mother's mother or anyone's grandmother.
You were Mary, widow of William, and no matriarch,
yet smoldering to the end with frustrate life,
ideas nobody listened to, least of all my father.
One summer night you sat with my sister and me
in the wooden glider long after twilight,
holding us there with streams of pent-up words.
You could quote every poet I had ever heard of,
had read *The Opium Eater*, Amiel and Bernard Shaw,
your green eyes looked clenched against opposition.

You married straight out of the convent school,
your background was country, you left an unperformed
typescript of a play about Burr and Hamilton,
you were impotent and brilliant, no one cared
about your mind, you might have ended
elsewhere than in that glider
reciting your unwritten novels to the children.

2. Hattie Rice Rich

Your sweetness of soul was a mystery to me,
you who slip-covered chairs, glued broken china,
lived out of a wardrobe trunk in our guestroom
summer and fall, then took the Pullman train
in your darkblue dress and straw hat, to Alabama,
shuttling half-yearly between your son and daughter.
Your sweetness of soul was a convenience for everyone,
how you rose with the birds and children, boiled your own egg,
fished for hours on a pier, your umbrella spread,
took the street-car downtown shopping
endlessly for your son's whims, the whims of genius,
kept your accounts in ledgers, wrote letters daily.
All through World War Two the forbidden word
Jewish was barely uttered in your son's house;
your anger flared over inscrutable things.
Once I saw you crouched on the guestroom bed,
knuckles blue-white around the bedpost, sobbing
your one brief memorable scene of rebellion:
you didn't want to go back South that year.
You were never "Grandmother Rich" but "Anana";
you had money of your own but you were homeless,
Hattie, widow of Samuel, and no matriarch,
dispersed among the children and grandchildren.

3. Granddaughter

Easier to encapsulate your lives
in a slide-show of impressions given and taken,
to play the child or victim, the projectionist,

easier to invent a script for each of you,
myself still at the center,
than to write words in which you might have found
yourselves, looked up at me and said
"Yes, I was like that; but I was something more. . . ."
Danville, Virginia; Vicksburg, Mississippi;
the "war between the states" a living memory
its aftermath the plague-town closing
its gates, trying to cure itself with poisons.
I can almost touch that little town. . . .
a little white town rimmed with Negroes,
making a deep shadow on the whiteness.
Born a white woman, Jewish or of curious mind
—twice an outsider, still believing in inclusion—
in those defended hamlets of half-truth
broken in two by one strange idea,
"blood" the all-powerful, awful theme—
what were the lessons to be learned? If I believe
the daughter of one of you—Amnesia was the answer.

1980

The Spirit of Place

—for Michelle Cliff

I.

Over the hills in Shutesbury, Leverett
driving with you in spring   road
like a streambed unwinding downhill
fiddlehead ferns uncurling
spring peepers ringing sweet and cold

•

while we talk yet again
of dark and light, of blackness, whiteness, numbness
rammed through the heart like a stake
trying to pull apart the threads
from the dried blood of the old murderous uncaring

halting on bridges in bloodlight
where the freshets call out freedom
to frog-thrilling swamp, skunk-cabbage
trying to sense the conscience of these hills

knowing how the single-minded, pure
solutions bleached and dessicated
within their perfect flasks

for it was not enough to be New England
as every event since has testified:
New England's a shadow-country, always was

it was not enough to be for abolition
while the spirit of the masters
flickered in the abolitionist's heart

it was not enough to name ourselves anew
while the spirit of the masters
calls the freedwoman to forget the slave

With whom do you believe your lot is cast?
If there's a conscience in these hills
it hurls that question

unquenched, relentless, to our ears
wild and witchlike
ringing every swamp

II.

The mountain laurel in bloom
constructed like needlework

tiny half-pulled stitches piercing
flushed and stippled petals

here in these woods it grows wild
midsummer moonrise turns it opal
the night breathes with its clusters
protected species

meaning endangered
Here in these hills
this valley   we have felt
a kind of freedom

planting the soil   have known
hours of a calm, intense and mutual solitude
reading and writing
trying to clarify   connect

past and present   near and far
the Alabama quilt
the Botswana basket
history   the dark crumble

of last year's compost
filtering softly through your living hand
but here as well we face
instantaneous violence   ambush   male

dominion on a back road
to escape in a locked car   windows shut
skimming the ditch   your split-second
survival reflex taking on the world

as it is   not as we wish it
as it is   not as we work for it
to be

III.

Strangers are an endangered species

•

In Emily Dickinson's house in Amherst
cocktails are served   the scholars
gather in celebration
their pious or clinical legends
festoon the walls like imitations
of period patterns

　　(. . . *and, as I feared, my "life" was made a "victim"*)

The remnants pawed   the relics
the cult assembled in the bedroom

and you   whose teeth were set on edge by churches
resist your shrine
　　　　　　　　escape
　　　　　　　　　　are found
nowhere
　　　　unless in words
　　　　　　　　　(your own)

　　All we are strangers—dear—The world is not
　　acquainted with us, because we are not acquainted
　　with her. And Pilgrims!—Do you hesitate? and
　　Soldiers oft—some of us victors, but those I do
　　not see tonight owing to the smoke.—We are hungry,
　　and thirsty, sometimes—We are barefoot—and cold—

This place is large enough for both of us
the river-fog will do for privacy
this is my third and last address to you

with the hands of a daughter I would cover you
from all intrusion   even my own
saying   rest to your ghost

with the hands of a sister I would leave your hands
open or closed as they prefer to lie
and ask no more of who or why or wherefore

　　●

with the hands of a mother I would close the door
on the rooms you've left behind
and silently pick up my fallen work

IV.

The river-fog will do for privacy
on the low road a breath
here, there, a cloudiness floating on the blacktop

sunflower heads turned black and bowed
the seas of corn a stubble
the old routes flowing north, if not to freedom

no human figure now in sight
(with whom do you believe your lot is cast?)
only the functional figure of the scarecrow

the cut corn, ground to shreds, heaped in a shape
like an Indian burial mound
a haunted-looking, ordinary thing

The work of winter starts fermenting in my head
how with the hands of a lover or a midwife
to hold back till the time is right

force nothing, be unforced
accept no giant miracles of growth
by counterfeit light

trust roots, allow the days to shrink
give credence to these slender means
wait without sadness and with grave impatience

here in the north where winter has a meaning
where the heaped colors suddenly go ashen
where nothing is promised

•

learn what an underground journey
has been, might have to be; speak in a winter code
let fog, sleet, translate; wind, carry them.

V.

Orion plunges like a drunken hunter
over the Mohawk Trail   a parallelogram
slashed with two cuts of steel

A night so clear that every constellation
stands out from an undifferentiated cloud
of stars, a kind of aura

All the figures up there look violent to me
as a pogrom on Christmas Eve in some old country
I want our own earth   not the satellites, our

world as it is   if not as it might be
then as it is: male dominion, gangrape, lynching, pogrom
the Mohawk wraiths in their tracts of leafless birch

watching: will we do better?
The tests I need to pass are prescribed by the spirits
of place   who understand travel but not amnesia

The world as it is: not as her users boast
damaged beyond reclamation by their using
Ourselves as we are   in these painful motions

of staying cognizant: some part of us always
out beyond ourselves
knowing   knowing   knowing

Are we all in training for something we don't name?
to exact reparation for things
done long ago to us and to those who did not

•

survive what was done to them   whom we ought to honor
with grief   with fury   with action
On a pure night   on a night when pollution

seems absurdity when the undamaged planet seems to turn
like a bowl of crystal in black ether
they are the piece of us that lies out there
knowing   knowing   knowing

1980

Frame

Winter twilight. She comes out of the lab-
oratory, last class of the day
a pile of notebooks slung in her knapsack, coat
zipped high against the already swirling
evening sleet. The wind is wicked and the
busses slower than usual. On her mind
is organic chemistry and the issue
of next month's rent and will it be possible to
bypass the professor with the coldest eyes
to get a reference for graduate school,
and whether any of them, even those who smile
can see, looking at her, a biochemist
or a marine biologist, which of the faces
can she trust to see her at all, either today
or in any future. The busses are worm-slow in the
quickly gathering dark. *I don't know her. I am
standing though somewhere just outside the frame
of all this, trying to see.* At her back
the newly finished building suddenly looks
like shelter, it has glass doors, lighted halls
presumably heat. The wind is wicked. She throws a
glance down the street, sees no bus coming and runs
up the newly constructed steps into the newly

constructed hallway. *I am standing all this time*
just beyond the frame, trying to see. She runs
her hand through the crystals of sleet about to melt
on her hair. She shifts the weight of the books
on her back. It isn't warm here exactly but it's
out of that wind. Through the glass
door panels she can watch for the bus through the thickening
weather. Watching so, she is not
watching for the white man who watches the building
who has been watching her. This is Boston 1979.
I am standing somewhere at the edge of the frame
watching the man, we are both white, who watches the building
telling her to move on, get out of the hallway.
I can hear nothing because I am not supposed to be
present but I can see her gesturing
out toward the street at the wind-raked curb
I see her drawing her small body up
against the implied charges. The man
goes away. Her body is different now.
It is holding together with more than a hint of fury
and more than a hint of fear. She is smaller, thinner
more fragile-looking than I am. *But I am not supposed to be*
there. I am just outside the frame
of this action when the anonymous white man
returns with a white police officer. Then she starts
to leave into the windraked night but already
the policeman is going to work, the handcuffs are on her
wrists he is throwing her down his knee has gone into
her breast he is dragging her down the stairs *I am unable*
to hear a sound of all this all that I know is what
I can see from this position there is no soundtrack
to go with this and I understand at once
it is meant to be in silence that this happens
in silence that he pushes her into the car
banging her head in silence that she cries out
in silence that she tries to explain she was only
waiting for a bus
in silence that he twists the flesh of her thigh

with his nails in silence that her tears begin to flow
that she pleads with the other policeman as if
he could be trusted to see her at all
in silence that in the precinct she refuses to give her name
in silence that they throw her into the cell
in silence that she stares him
straight in the face in silence that he sprays her
in her eyes with Mace in silence that she sinks her teeth
into his hand in silence that she is charged
with trespass assault and battery in
silence that at the sleet-swept corner her bus
passes without stopping and goes on
in silence. *What I am telling you*
is told by a white woman who they will say
was never there. I say I am there.

1980

Turning the Wheel

1. *Location*

No room for nostalgia here. What would it look like?
The imitation of a ghost mining town,
the movie-set façade of a false Spanish
arcade, the faceless pueblo
with the usual faceless old woman grinding corn?
It's all been done. Acre on acre
of film locations disguised as Sears,
Safeway, the Desert National Bank,
Fashion Mall, Sun Valley Waterbeds.
Old people, rich, pass on in cloistered stucco
tiled and with fountains; poor, at Golden Acres
Trailer Ranch for Adult Seniors, at the edge of town,
close by the Reassembled Church of Latter-Day
Saints and a dozen motels called Mountain View.

The mountains are on view from everywhere
in this desert: this poor, conquered, bulldozed desert
overridden like a hold-out
enemy village. Nostalgia for the desert
will soon draw you to the Desert Museum
or off on an unpaved track to stare at one saguaro
—velvety, pleated, from a distance graceful—
closer-on, shot through with bullet holes
and seeming to give the finger to it all.

2. *Burden Baskets*

False history gets made all day, any day,
the truth of the new is never on the news
False history gets written every day
and by some who should know better:
the lesbian archaeologist watches herself
sifting her own life out from the shards she's piecing,
asking the clay all questions but her own.
Yet suddenly for once the standard version
splits open to something shocking, unintentional.
In the elegant Southwest Museum, no trace of bloodshed
or broken treaty. But, behind glass, these baskets
woven for the young women's puberty dances
still performed among the still surviving
Apache people;   filled with offerings:
cans of diet Pepsi, peanut brittle,
Cracker Jack, Hershey bars
piled there, behind glass, without notation
in the anthropologist's typewritten text
which like a patient voice tired of explaining
goes on to explain a different method of weaving.

3. *Hohokam*

Nostalgia is only amnesia turned around.
I try to pierce through to a prehistoric culture
the museum says were known as *those who have ceased.*
I try to imagine them, before the Hopi

or Navaho, *those who have ceased*
but they draw back, an archetypal blur.
Did they leave behind for Pima or Navaho
something most precious, now archaic,
more than a faceless woman grinding corn?
Those who have ceased is amnesia-language:
no more to be said of them. Nobody wants
to see their faces or hear what they were about.
I try to imagine a desert-shamaness
bringing water to fields of squash, maize and cotton
but where the desert herself is half-eroded
half-flooded by a million jets of spray
to conjure a rich white man's paradise
the shamaness could well have withdrawn her ghost.

4. *Self-hatred*

In Colcha embroidery, I learn,
women use ravelled yarn from old wool blankets
to trace out scenes on homespun woollen sacks—
our ancient art of making out of nothing—
or is it making the old life serve the new?
The impact of Christian culture, it is written,
and other influences, have changed the patterns.
(*Once they were birds perhaps*, I think; *or serpents.*)
Example: here we have a scene of flagellants,
each whip is accurately self-directed.
To understand colonization is taking me
years. I stuck my loaded needle
into the coarse squares of the sack, I smoothed
the stylized pattern on my knee with pride.
I also heard them say my own designs
were childlike, primitive, obscene.
What rivets me to history is seeing
arts of survival turned
to rituals of self-hatred. This
is colonization. Unborn sisters,
look back on us in mercy where we failed ourselves,

see us not one-dimensional but with
the past as your steadying and corrective lens.

5. *Particularity*

In search of the desert witch, the shamaness
forget the archetypes, forget the dark
and lithic profile, do not scan the clouds
massed on the horizon, violet and green,
for her icon, do not pursue
the ready-made abstraction, do not peer for symbols.
So long as you want her faceless, without smell
or voice, so long as she does not squat
to urinate, or scratch herself, so long
as she does not snore beneath her blanket
or grimace as she grasps the stone-cold
grinding stone at dawn
so long as she does not have her own peculiar
face, slightly wall-eyed or with a streak
of topaz lightning in the blackness
of one eye, so long as she does not limp
so long as you try to simplify her meaning
so long as she merely symbolizes power
she is kept helpless and conventional
her true power routed backward
into the past, we cannot touch or name her
and, barred from participation by those who need her
she stifles in unspeakable loneliness.

6. *Apparition*

If she appears, hands ringed with rings
you have dreamed about, if on her large fingers
jasper and sardonyx and agate smolder
if she is wearing shawls woven in fire
and blood, if she is wearing shawls
of undyed fiber, yellowish
if on her neck are hung
obsidian and silver, silver and turquoise
if she comes skirted like a Christian

her hair combed back by missionary fingers
if she sits offering her treasure by the road
to spare a brother's or an uncle's dignity
or if she sits pretending
to weave or grind or do some other thing
for the appeasement of the ignorant
if she is the famous potter
whose name confers honor on certain vessels
if she is wrist-deep in mud and shawled in dust
and wholly anonymous
look at her closely if you dare
do not assume you know those cheekbones
or those eye-sockets; or that still-bristling hair.

7. *Mary Jane Colter, 1904*

My dear Mother and Sister:
                              I have been asked
to design a building in the Hopi style
at the Grand Canyon. As you know
in all my travels for Mr. Harvey
and the Santa Fe Railroad, I have thought this the greatest
sight in the Southwest—in our land entire.
I am here already, trying to make a start.
I cannot tell you with what elation
this commission has filled me. I regret to say
it will mean I cannot come home to St. Paul
as I hoped, this spring. I am hoping this may lead
to other projects here, of equal grandeur.
(Do you understand? I want this glory.
I want to place my own conception
and that of the Indians whose land this was
at the edge of this incommensurable thing.)
I know my life seems shaky, unreliable
to you. When this is finished I promise you
to come home to St. Paul and teach. You will never lack
for what I can give you. Your affectionate
daughter and sister,
                    Mary.

8. *Turning the Wheel*

The road to the great canyon always feels
like that road and no other
the highway to a fissure   to the female core
of a continent
Below Flagstaff even   the rock erosions wear
a famous handwriting
the river's still prevailing signature

Seeing those rocks   that road   in dreams   I know
it is happening again   as twice while waking
I am travelling to the edge   to meet the face
of annihilating and impersonal time
stained in the colors of a woman's genitals
outlasting every transient violation
a face that is strangely intimate to me

Today I turned the wheel   refused that journey
I was feeling too alone on the open plateau
of piñon juniper   world beyond time
of rockflank spread around me   too alone
and too filled with you   with whom I talked for hours
driving up from the desert   though you were far away
as I talk to you all day   whatever day

1981

Poems
1982–1983

For the Record

The clouds and the stars didn't wage this war
the brooks gave no information
if the mountain spewed stones of fire into the river
it was not taking sides
the raindrop faintly swaying under the leaf
had no political opinions

and if here or there a house
filled with backed-up raw sewage
or poisoned those who lived there
with slow fumes, over years
the houses were not at war
nor did the tinned-up buildings

intend to refuse shelter
to homeless old women and roaming children
they had no policy to keep them roaming
or dying, no, the cities were not the problem
the bridges were non-partisan
the freeways burned, but not with hatred

Even the miles of barbed-wire
stretched around crouching temporary huts
designed to keep the unwanted
at a safe distance, out of sight
even the boards that had to absorb
year upon year, so many human sounds

so many depths of vomit, tears
slow-soaking blood
had not offered themselves for this
The trees didn't volunteer to be cut into boards
nor the thorns for tearing flesh
Look around at all of it

and ask whose signature
is stamped on the orders, traced
in the corner of the building plans
Ask where the illiterate, big-bellied
women were, the drunks and crazies,
the ones you fear most of all: ask where you were.

1983

Education of a Novelist

—Italicized lines
quoted from Ellen
Glasgow's autobiography,
The Woman Within.

I

Looking back   trying to decipher
yourself and Lizzie Jones:
                    We were strange companions, but
that everyone knew us: a dark
lean, eager colored woman
and a small, pale, eager little girl
roaming together, hand-in-hand

Waking early, Mammy and I
would be dressed before the family had risen
spurred on by an inborn love
                    of adventure
a vital curiosity
            . . . visiting
the neighbors and and the neighbors' cooks and *with the neighbors'*
maids sweeping the brick pavement
                        and the apothecary
and the friendly light-colored letter-carrier

•

But when you made one visit to the almshouse
Mammy was reprimanded

II

> *I revolted from sentimentality*
> *less because it was false than because*
> *it was cruel . . .*
>   In the country, later
> the Black artist spent her genius on the white children
> *Mammy was with us; we were all happy together*
> (I revolted from sentimentality   when it suited me)
>
> *She would dress us as gypsies, darken*
> *our faces with burnt cork*
>   *We would start*
> *on a long journey, telling fortunes*
> *wherever we came to a farm or a Negro cabin*
> *I was always the one who would*
> *think up the most exciting fortunes*
>   (I, too, was always the one)

III

> *Where or how I learned to read*
> (you boast so proudly)   *I could never*
> *remember   After supper*
> *in front of the fire, undressing by candlelight*
> *Mammy and I would take up and spin out*
> *the story left from the evening before*
>
> *Nobody ever taught me to read*
>   (Nobody had to,
> it was your birthright, Ellen.)
>
> *"As soon as I learn my letters,*
> *Mammy, I'm going to teach you yours"*
>   (But you never taught her.)

•

IV

Givens, Ellen.   That we'd *pick out our way*
through the Waverly novels
that our childish, superior fire
was destined for fortune

even though female   deaf   or lame
dewomanized   The growing suspicion
haunting the growing life

the sense of exile in a hostile world
how do we use that?
                         and for what?
                                  with whom?

Givens.   The pale skin, the eager look
the fact of having been known
                         by everyone
our childish, superior fire, and all
I was always the one . . .
                         Deafness finally drives you
here, there, to specialists in Europe
for hardening of the Eustachian tube

Finding no cure you build
a wall of deceptive gaiety   to shield your pain:
That I, who was winged for flying, should be
wounded and caged!

V

Lizzie Jones vanishes.   Her trace is lost.
She, who was winged for flying

                         Where at the end
of the nineteenth century   you ask
could one find the Revolution?

In what mean streets and alleys of the South
was it then lying in ambush?   Though I suffered
with the world's suffering . . .
                              "As soon
as I learn my letters, Mammy,
I'm going to teach you yours"
                              but by your own admission
you never did

Where at the end of the twentieth century
does the Revolution find us
in what streets and alleys, north or south
is it now lying in ambush?
                              It's not enough
using your words to damn you, Ellen:
they could have been my own:
                              this criss-cross
map of kept and broken promises
                              I was always the one

1983

Upcountry

The silver shadow   where the line falls grey
and pearly   the unborn villages quivering
under the rock   the snail   travelling the crevice
the furred, flying white insect like a tiny
intelligence lacing the air
this woman whose lips lie parted
after long speech
her white hair unrestrained

All that you never paid
or have with difficulty paid
attention to

•

Change and be forgiven!   the roots of the forest
muttered   but you tramped through   guilty
unable to take forgiveness   neither do you
give mercy

She is asleep now   dangerous   her mind
slits the air like silk   travels faster than sound
like scissors flung into the next century

Even as you watch for the trout's hooked stagger
across the lake   the crack of light and the crumpling bear
her mind was on them first
                              when forgiveness ends
her love means danger

1983

When/Then

Tell us
        how we'll be together
                        in that time
patch of sun on a gritty floor; an old newspaper, torn
for toilet paper and coughed-up scum   Don't talk, she said

when we still love but are no longer young

they bring you a raw purple stick and say
it is one of her fingers;   it could be
                              Tell us
about aging, what it costs, how women
have loved forty, fifty years
                        enamel basin, scraped
down to the bare iron   some ashen hairs   red fluid
they say is her blood   how can you tell?

●

Tell us about the gardens we will keep, the milk
we'll drink from our own goats

                              she needs
anti-biotics they say which will be given
when you name names   they show you her fever chart

Tell us about community   the joy
of coming to rest

                    among women

                                who will love us

you choose between your community
and her   later others
will come through the cell   not all of them will love you
whichever way you choose

Don't talk, she said   (you will learn to hear
only her voice when they close in on you)   Don't talk

Why are you telling us this?

                              patch of sun on a gritty
floor, bad dreams, a torn newspaper, someone's blood
in a scraped basin . . .

1983

In the Wake of Home

1.

You sleep in a room with bluegreen curtains
posters   a pile of animals on the bed
A woman and a man who love you
and each other   slip the door ajar
you are almost asleep   they crouch in turn
to stroke your hair   you never wake

●

This happens every night for years.
This never happened.

2.

Your lips   steady   never say
It should have been this way
That's not what you say
You   so carefully not asking, *Why?*
Your eyes   looking straight in mine
remind me of a woman's
auburn hair   my mother's hair
but you never saw that hair

The family coil   so twisted, tight and loose
anyone trying to leave
has to strafe the field
burn the premises down

3.

The home houses
mirages   memory fogs the kitchen panes
the rush-hour traffic outside
has the same old ebb and flow
Out on the darkening block
somebody calls you home
night after night   then never again
Useless for you to know
they tried to do what they could
before they left for good

4.

The voice that used to call you home
has gone off on the wind
beaten into thinnest air
whirling down other streets
or maybe the mouth was burnt to ash
maybe the tongue was torn out

brownlung has stolen the breath
or fear has stolen the breath
maybe under another name
it sings on AM radio:
And if you knew, what would you know?

5.

But you will be drawn to places
where generations lie
side by side with each other:
fathers, mothers and children
in the family prayerbook
or the country burying-ground
You will hack your way back through the bush
to the *Jodensavanne*
where the gravestones are black with mould
You will stare at old family albums
with their smiles   their resemblances
you will want to believe that nobody
wandered off   became strange
no woman dropped her baby and ran
no father took off for the hills
no axe splintered the door
—that once at least it was all in order
and nobody came to grief

6.

Any time you go back
where absence began
the kitchen faucet sticks in a way you know
you have to pull the basement door
in before drawing the bolt
the last porch-step is still loose
the water from the tap
is the old drink of water
Any time you go back
the familiar underpulse

will start its throbbing: *Home, home!*
and the hole torn and patched over
will gape unseen again

7.

Even where love has run thin
the child's soul musters strength
calling on dust-motes   song on the radio
closet-floor of galoshes
stray cat   piles of autumn leaves
whatever comes along
—the rush of purpose to make a life
worth living past abandonment
building the layers up again
over the torn hole   filling in

8.

And what of the stern and faithful aunt
the fierce grandmother   the anxious sister
the good teacher   the one
who stood at the crossing when you had to cross
the woman hired to love you
the skeleton who held out a crust
the breaker of rules   the one
who is neither a man nor a woman
who warmed the liquid vein of life
and day after day whatever the need
handed it on to you?
You who did and had to do
so much for yourself   this was done for you
by someone who did what they could
when others left for good

9.

You imagine an alley   a little kingdom
where the mother-tongue is spoken
a village of shelters   woven

or sewn of hides   in a long-ago way
a shanty standing up
at the edge of sharecropped fields
a tenement where life is seized by the teeth
a farm battened down on snowswept plains
a porch with rubber-plant and glider
on a steep city street
You imagine the people would all be there
fathers mothers and children
the ones you were promised would all be there
eating   arguing   working
trying to get on with life
you imagine this used to be
for everyone   everywhere

10.

What if I told you your home
is this continent of the homeless
of children sold   taken by force
driven from their mothers' land
killed by their mothers to save from capture
—this continent of changed names and mixed-up blood
of languages tabooed
diasporas unrecorded
undocumented refugees
underground railroads   trails of tears
What if I tell you your home
is this planet of warworn children
women and children standing in line or milling
endlessly calling each others' names
What if I tell you, you are not different
it's the family albums that lie
—will any of this comfort you
and how should this comfort you?

11.

The child's soul carries on
in the wake of home

building a complicated house
a tree-house without a tree
finding places for everything
the song   the stray cat   the skeleton
The child's soul musters strength
where the holes were torn
but there are no miracles:
even children become exhausted
And how shall they comfort each other
who have come young to grief?
Who will number the grains of loss
and what would comfort be?

1983

North American Time

I

When my dreams showed signs
of becoming
politically correct
no unruly images
escaping beyond borders
when walking in the street I found my
themes cut out for me
knew what I would not report
for fear of enemies' usage
then I began to wonder

II

Everything we write
will be used against us
or against those we love.
These are the terms,
take them or leave them.

Poetry never stood a chance
of standing outside history.
One line typed twenty years ago
can be blazed on a wall in spraypaint
to glorify art as detachment
or torture of those we
did not love but also
did not want to kill

We move   but our words stand
become responsible
for more than we intended

and this is verbal privilege

III

Try sitting at a typewriter
one calm summer evening
at a table by a window
in the country, try pretending
your time does not exist
that you are simply you
that the imagination simply strays
like a great moth, unintentional
try telling yourself
you are not accountable
to the life of your tribe
the breath of your planet

IV

It doesn't matter what you think.
Words are found responsible
all you can do is choose them
or choose
to remain silent.   Or, you never had a choice,
which is why the words that do stand
are responsible

●

and this is verbal privilege

V

Suppose you want to write
of a woman braiding
another woman's hair—
straight down, or with beads and shells
in three-strand plaits or corn-rows—
you had better know the thickness
the length   the pattern
why she decides to braid her hair
how it is done to her   /
what country it happens in
what else happens in that country

You have to know these things

VI

Poet, sister: words—
whether we like it or not—
stand in a time of their own.
No use protesting   *I wrote that
before Kollontai was exiled
Rosa Luxembourg, Malcolm,
Anna Mae Aquash, murdered,
before Treblinka, Birkenau,
Hiroshima, before Sharpeville,
Biafra, Bangla Desh, Boston,
Atlanta, Soweto, Beirut, Assam*
—those faces, names of places
sheared from the almanac
of North American time

VII

I am thinking this in a country
where words are stolen out of mouths
as bread is stolen out of mouths

where poets don't go to jail
for being poets, but for being
dark-skinned, female, poor.
I am writing this in a time
when anything we write
can be used against those we love
where the context is never given
though we try to explain, over and over
For the sake of poetry at least
I need to know these things

VIII

Sometimes, gliding at night
in a plane over New York City
I have felt like some messenger
called to enter, called to engage
this field of light and darkness.
A grandiose idea, born of flying.
But underneath the grandiose idea
is the thought that what I must engage
after the plane has raged into the tarmac
after climbing my old stairs, sitting down
at my old window
is meant to break my heart and reduce me to silence.

IX

In North America time stumbles on
without moving, only releasing
a certain North American pain.
Julia de Burgos wrote:
That my grandfather was a slave
is my grief; had he been a master
that would have been my shame.
A poet's words, hung over a door
in North America, in the year
nineteen-eighty-three.
The almost-full moon rises
timelessly speaking of change

out of the Bronx, the Harlem River
the drowned towns of the Quabbin
the pilfered burial mounds
the toxic swamps, the testing-grounds

and I start to speak again.

1983

Notes

The Tourist and the Town. The pronouns in the third section were originally masculine. But the tourist was a woman—myself—and I never saw her as anything else. In 1953, when the poem was written, a notion of male experience as universal prevailed which made the feminine pronoun suspect, or merely "personal." In this poem, as in "Afterward," I later altered the pronouns because they alter, for me, the dimensions of the poem.

Villa Adriana. The summer palace built by the Emperor Hadrian for his favorite boy lover, Antinoüs. In "Antinoüs: The Diaries" I let the young man speak for me.

The Snow Queen. Hans Christian Andersen's tale was the point of departure.

The Diamond Cutters. Thirty years later I have trouble with the informing metaphor of this poem. I was trying, in my twenties, to write about the craft of poetry. But I was drawing, quite ignorantly, on the long tradition of domination, according to which the precious resource is yielded up into the hands of the dominator as if by a natural event. The enforced and exploited labor of actual Africans in actual diamond mines was invisible to me, and therefore invisible in the poem, which does not take responsibility for its own metaphor. I note this here because this kind of metaphor is still widely accepted, and I still have to struggle against it in my work.

SNAPSHOTS OF A DAUGHTER-IN-LAW

Snapshots of a Daughter-in-Law. The lines in Part 7 beginning "To have in this uncertain world some stay" were written by Mary Wollstonecraft in *Thoughts on the Education of Daughters* (London, 1787).

329

NECESSITIES OF LIFE

In the Woods. The first line is borrowed and translated from the Dutch poet, J. C. Bloem.

I Am in Danger—Sir—. See *The Letters of Emily Dickinson,* Thomas Johnson and Theodora Ward, eds., Vol. 2 (Cambridge: Harvard University Press, 1958), p. 409.

LEAFLETS

Orion. One or two phrases suggested by Gottfried Benn's essay, "Artists and Old Age," in *Primal Vision: Selected Writings,* ed. E. B. Ashton. (New York: New Directions, 1960).

Charleston in the Eighteen-Sixties. See Mary Boykin Chesnut, *A Diary from Dixie,* Ben Ames Williams, ed. (Boston: Houghton Mifflin, 1963).

For a Russian Poet. Part 3 is based on an account by the poet Natalya Gorbanevskaya of a protest action against the Soviet invasion of Czechoslovakia. Gorbanevskaya was later held, and bore a child, in a "penal mental institution" for her political activities. See "For a Sister," p. 175.

Poem of Women. This poem and "White Night" (p. 196) were adapted from the Yiddish with the aid of transliterated versions and prose translations provided by Eliezer Greenberg and Irving Howe, in whose anthology, *A Treasury of Yiddish Poetry* (New York: Holt, Rinehart and Winston, 1969), these first appeared.

Leaflets. "The love of a fellow-creature in all its fullness consists simply in the ability to say to him, 'What are you going through?' "—Simone Weil.

The Observer. Suggested by a brief newspaper account of the fieldwork of Dian Fossey. She has more recently written of her own observations in *Gorillas in the Mist* (Boston: Houghton Mifflin, 1983).

Ghazals: Homage to Ghalib. This poem began to be written after I read Aijaz Ahmad's literal English versions of the Urdu poetry of Mirza Ghalib (1797–1869). While the structure and metrics of the classical *ghazal* form used by Ghalib are much stricter than mine, I adhered to his use of a minimum five couplets to a *ghazal*, each couplet being autonomous and independent of the others. The continuity and unity flow from the associations and images playing back and forth among the couplets in any single *ghazal*. The poems are dated as I wrote them, during a month in the summer of 1968. Although I was a contributor to Ahmad's *The Ghazals of Ghalib* (New York: Columbia University Press, 1971), the *ghazals* here are not translations but original poems.

POEMS 1950–1974

The first four poems in this section were "lost" for a long time; I had even forgotten their existence. "The Prisoners," "The House at the Cascades," and "Night" first appeared in *The Harvard Advocate*, and "At the Jewish New Year" in *The New Yorker*. "Dien Bien Phu" appeared in *Nimrod*.

From an Old House in America. Part 4: The first line is borrowed from Emily Brontë's poem, "Stanzas."
Part 7: Many African women went into labor and gave birth on the slave-ships of the Middle Passage, chained for the duration of the voyage to the dying or the dead.
Part 11: *Datura* is a poisonous hallucinogenic weed with a spiky green pod and a white flower; also known as jimson-weed, or deadly nightshade.

THE DREAM OF A COMMON LANGUAGE

Paula Becker to Clara Westhoff. Some phrases in this poem are quoted from actual diaries and letters of Paula Modersohn-Becker, which were shown me in unpublished translations by Liselotte Glozer. Since then, an annotated translation of the manuscripts has been published by Diane Radycki: *The Letters and Journals of Paula Modersohn-Becker* (Metuchen, N.J.: Scarecrow Press, 1980).

A WILD PATIENCE HAS TAKEN ME THIS FAR

Integrity. To my knowledge, this word was first introduced in a feminist context by Janice Raymond in her essay, "The Illusion of Androgyny," *Quest: A Feminist Quarterly*, Vol. 2, No. 1 (Summer 1975).

Culture and Anarchy. The title is stolen from Matthew Arnold's collection of essays by the same name, first published in London, 1869. The sources for the voices of the nineteenth-century white women heard in this poem are as follows: Diaries of Susan B. Anthony, 1861; letter from Anthony to her sister, 1883, both in Ida Husted Harper, *The Life and Work of Susan B. Anthony* (Indianapolis: Bowes-Merrill, 1899); Jane Addams, *Twenty Years at Hull House* (New York: Macmillan, 1926); Elizabeth Barrett-Browning, letter to Anna Brownell Jameson, 1852, in *The Letters of Elizabeth Barrett Browning* ed., Frederick Kenyon, Vol. 2 (New York: Macmillan, 1898); Ida Husted Harper, introduction to Susan B. Anthony and Ida Husted Harper, *The History of Woman Suffrage*, Vol. 4 (1902). Elizabeth Cady Stanton, speech "On Solitude of Self," in Anthony and Harper, *The History of Woman Suffrage*, Vol. 4; Elizabeth Cady Stanton, letter to Susan B. Anthony, in Harper, *The Life and Work of Susan B. Anthony*, Vol. 1.

For Julia in Nebraska. Epigraph quoted from the Willa Cather Educational Foundation, Historical Landmark Council, marker at the intersection of Highways 281 and 4, fourteen miles north of Red Cloud, Nebraska.

Mother-in-Law. It has been suggested to me that the lines "I am trying to tell you, I envy/the people in mental hospitals their freedom" add to a stockpile of false images of mental patients' incarceration—images which help perpetuate their pain and the system which routinely drugs, curbs, "constrains," electroshocks, and surgically experiments on them. The woman speaking in the poem speaks, of course, out of her own frustration and despair, and so the lines are bitterly ironic; but I agree with my critics that in a world eager both to romanticize and to torture mental patients, such clichés must be used, if at all, with utmost concern for the realities underlying them.

Heroines. See Gerda Lerner: "The history of notable women is the history of exceptional, even deviant women, and does not describe the experience and history of the mass of women." In Gerda Lerner, "Placing Women in History: Definitions and Challenges," *The Majority Finds Its Past* (New York: Oxford University Press, 1979).

Grandmothers. Part 3: Italicized lines are quoted from Lillian Smith, *Killers of the Dream* (New York: Norton, 1961), p. 39.

The Spirit of Place. Italicized passages in Part 3 are from *The Letters of Emily Dickinson*, Thomas Johnson and Theodora Ward, eds. (Cambridge: Harvard University Press, 1958), specifically, from Letter 154 to Susan Gilbert (June 1854) and Letter 203 to Catherine Scott Anthon Turner (March 1859).

Turning the Wheel. Part 3: The Hohokam were a prehistoric farming culture who developed irrigation canals in southern Arizona and southwestern New Mexico between about 300 B.C. and C.E. 1400. The word *hohokam* is Pima and is translated variously as "those who have ceased" or "those who were used up." See Emil W. Haury, *The Hohokam, Desert Farmers and Craftsmen* (sic) (Tucson: University of Arizona Press, 1976). Part 7: The letter is a poetic fiction, based upon reading Virginia Grattan's *Mary Colter, Builder upon the Red Earth* (Flagstaff, Ariz.: Northland Press, 1980). Mary E. J. Colter studied design and architecture in order to support her mother and younger sister upon her father's death. She taught art in a St. Paul, Minnesota, high school for fifteen years before starting to work as a decorator for the Fred Harvey Company and the Santa Fe Railroad. Soon she was in charge of both exterior and interior design of hotels and restaurants from Chicago westward. At the height of her career she designed eight major buildings at the Grand Canyon, all of which are still standing. She never married. She drew consistently on American Indian arts and design in her work, and her collection of Hopi and

Navaho art can be seen at Mesa Verde Museum. Her life-work
—remarkable for a woman architect—was framed by the con-
tradiction that made it inseparable from the violation and ex-
propriation by white entrepreneurs of the original cultures she
respected and loved.

POEMS 1982–1983

In the Wake of Home. The Jodensavanne is an abandoned Jewish
settlement in Surinam whose ruins exist in a jungle on the Cas-
sipoera River.

North American Time. Julia de Burgos (1914–1953): Puerto
Rican poet and revolutionary, who died on the streets of New
York City.

My thanks to the journals in which some of these poems were
first published: *I-Kon, River Styx, The Boston Review.* "Up-
country" was originally published as a broadside by The Heyeck
Press.

Index

335

Three flesh Tunnels
we possess,
And allow To enter,
Large & small
missiles that explode,
Thousands of life deciding
atoms.